PREACHING TO THE CHOIR
REFLECTIONS FOR THE AQUINAS COMMUNITY

1999-2013

ANN M. GARRIDO

To: Hannah
w/gratitude
Ann Garrido
9-10-14

NEW PRIORY PRESS
EXPLORING THE DOMINICAN VISION

i

Production Editor: Albert Judy, O.P.; Cover Design: Susan Webb
Copyright © 2014 Dominican Province of St. Albert the Great (U.S.A.).
All rights reserved. Published by New Priory Press,
1910 South Ashland Avenue, Chicago, IL 60608   www.NewPrioryPress.com

Contents

Forward
by Donald J. Goergen, O.P.

In the Order of Preachers, after having proven oneself over time, an honor, a high honor, is sometimes bestowed on a theologian or preacher. For a theologian, this honor is that of a Master of Sacred Theology, which goes back to a practice in the medieval university whereby one became a *magister*—one entitled to teach in his own right. A master preacher was so acknowledged or honored by the conferral of the title of Preacher General—someone whose preaching had proven itself in the arena of *orthopraxis*. This latter honor is no longer bestowed. However, if it still were, and if Ann Garrido were a formal member of the Order, she certainly would be so recognized.

Not unlike Catherine of Siena, Ann is a lay woman who was called into the service of Our Lord Jesus Christ. As a college student Ann spent nine months in Africa (Sierra Leone and Kenya). After college she went to teach for four years with the School Sisters of Notre Dame in Guam, where she married Michael and gave birth to their son Micah. Ann has given her life to ministry in the Church. In 1996 they moved to the States, to St. Louis, where she began theological studies. Having obtained a D.Min. in Preaching from the Aquinas Institute of Theology, she later directed that same program. Upon leaving full time ministry and the regular faculty at Aquinas Institute in 2013, having been both a professor and an administrator at the Aquinas Institute, Ann submitted this collection of preachings which she had given between 2001 and 2013. I myself had not heard Ann preach most of these since I was not myself at Aquinas Institute during all of that time, although previously she had been both a student of mine and later a colleague. But upon reading this collection, I felt it needed to be made available to a wider congregation.

Ann preached regularly at midday prayer at the school. Her congregation comprised students of theology, faculty, and staff. She herself was a member of that faculty. She gathered together this collection of preachings as a kind of expression of gratitude for what she had been given, not perhaps as fully aware of what she herself had given. So why make them more widely available?

Aware that preaching is an oral medium, I began to read the written texts, at first I suppose somewhat out of a sense of loyalty and friendship. As I read, my heart was stirred. These preachings spoke to me years after she had preached them. I began using them for spiritual reading, one a day. Each one spoke, came alive although having been delivered years before. These were not just occasional preachings. They were well crafted, gave witness to a sensitivity as to how words can be a channel of grace, and always, always, had a deep meaning the relevance of which extends beyond the occasion on which they were preached, although knowing that occasion allows one to appreciate them contextually as well as "for ages to come." Simply put, I invite you to partake of the Word that these preachings communicate—whether as a student of preaching or a preacher yourself, whether as someone desiring to deepen your own life in Christ, or whether as someone who may not have the luxury to hear preaching on a regular basis. Ann is a lay preacher and gives witness to the importance of lay preaching in the life of the Church.

Aware that each of us have been given the gift of the Spirit, and that as St. Paul indicates, to each is also given a manifestation of the Spirit for the common good (1 Cor 12: 7), and that to some is given the gift of preaching, to others other gifts, so these gifts are not for ourselves nor for a circle of friends, but for the community, the *ecclesia*. As in any preaching, some are moved by one thing, others by another, and some not at all, or someone is moved by a preaching that the preacher himself or herself thought to fall short of what they wanted it to be. So here, what each one receives will depend upon what each one needs, to what each one is open, to how the Spirit works invisibly in the hearer of the Word. The Church is simply the sphere of influence of the Holy Spirit and the Spirit blows where and how He will (Jn 3:8). The Spirit is the soul of the Church and the source of all preaching. In the end it is not we who preach but the Spirit who preaches from within us. So let the Spirit guide you where these preachings may take you. They are not a light to be hidden under a bushel basket (Mt 5: 14-16).

Thank you, Ann.

Introduction

For a couple of years, I was honored to assist Dan Harris with the Foundations of Preaching class at AI. I heard lots of wonderful, well-crafted stuff, but not infrequently would have to ask, "Who was that for?" These initial forays into preaching took place in our school chapel in front of four or five fellow theology students and myself. After hearing about the importance of being present at Sunday Mass or the evils of something like money laundering, I would have to ask, "Who among us did you have in mind when preparing that message? When you look out at us, what do you see?"

I had the privilege of preaching at Aquinas Institute for approximately 15 years. I started as a third year MDiv student and liked it so much I refused to stop. As you open this collection, I hope it is clear exactly what I saw when I looked out at "my congregation." The Aquinas worshipping community is comprised of people who make a daily effort to conform their lives to their most deeply held beliefs. They are regular Mass goers and I have never seen any evidence whatsoever of money laundering. They gamble, but only in the sense of committing themselves to the practice of their faith in quite a radical way, and most of them would not consider that a gamble. When I looked out at this community year after year, I saw generous, fun-loving, compassionate people, who—yes, occasionally hogged the single microwave for six minutes during peak lunch hour with their low-sodium soup or permafrost "Hot Pocket"—but never did so with malevolent intent. We frequently disagreed about how a program should be run or money should be spent, but I never had reason to doubt their charity. I hope that when you read these reflections, you are able to tell something about how much I loved this community, especially the little remnant that continued to gather weekly for midday prayer even as the practice went out of vogue.

When I took Theology of Preaching as a Doctorate of Ministry student, I remember Greg Heille holding up a volume of Karl Barth's *Church Dogmatics* and Catherine Hilkert's *Naming Grace* as the poles of two directions toward which we might walk as preachers: The first confronting the congregation with the otherness of the Word, illuminating the sharp contrast between God's will and their lives. The second naming the many ways in which God was already moving in a community, already present in the actions and words of people who are imperfect and needing challenge, but already so filled with grace. There are representations of both "Barthian" and "Hilkertian" preaching in this collection, but if I seem to tilt toward Hilkert it is because the setting demanded it. Lots of preachers might recognize when looking out at those present for liturgy, "Well, I'm preaching this to the choir." But I really was.

Much happened during my time at Aquinas–both within the school community and in the larger ecclesial and political spheres. I originally thought I would arrange the homilies following the liturgical year, but decided they might make more sense chronologically because of some of the very specific events in time that they reference. It really is true that good preaching sits at the juncture of not just a particular scripture and a particular community, but also a particular time. Preaching is kind of like Buddhist sand art. You put your whole heart and soul into the creation of something whose relevance may not last beyond sunset.

My habit has been to preach on one of the lectionary readings of the day, but not infrequently I was enamored with the saint of the day and chose something from one of their writings. If the preaching was on a scripture passage/s, I've only included the reference. If on the writing of a saint, I've included the text since it would be less familiar to the reader. I've limited this collection to reflections prepared exclusively for the Aquinas community with three exceptions–all events at which a good subsection of Aquinas was present. The collection isn't comprehensive; it got too long when I tried to include everything! But I think it is fairly representative. Michael Mascari once said to me that every preacher really only has five homilies that they keep re-working over and over again in some fashion or another. I think you'll find that true here. Indeed, I'd enjoy hearing what you think they are.

One note of clarification: many of the reflections make some mention of the "atrium." My years at Aquinas parallel precisely the years that I have been involved in the Catechesis of the Good Shepherd movement– a Montessori-based religious formation experience involving children ages three through twelve. I became involved in "CGS" in 1996–the year my son Micah turned one, the same yearI began graduate studies at Aquinas Institute. Alongside Aquinas, the CGS community been the most influential force in my own spiritual development and theological thought, and indeed, I do not even think of these two communities as distinct. For a deeper understanding of what CGS is about, see www.cgsusa.org.

I want to say thank you to the Aquinas community for giving me the privilege of being one of its preachers for such a sustained period of time. I would never have encountered the Word of God in such a meaningful way without this amazing group of faith-filled people.

Ann Garrido

1. *Aquinas Midday Prayer*
Mardi Gras–The Burying of the Alleluia
February 16, 1999

When Micah was just a little over a year old, maybe a year and a half, one night I had the radical idea that maybe I should start praying with him... you know, being a theology student and all. In some of my own studies, I had been reading about the child's innate relationship with God that longed to have space to express itself. So I sat down on his mattress on the floor as he lay down to go to sleep at night and I said to him, "Micah, is there anything you'd like to say to Jesus before you go to sleep tonight?" Now, mind you the kid hardly spoke more than 20 words at this point and I wasn't sure he was even going to know what I was talking about. But, he just kind of looked beyond me and said–very clearly and very intentionally–"Alleluia."

"Alleluia," the first prayer of a child.

I was quite stunned at the time, but now I think it shouldn't have surprised me. For when we listen to language as it first emerges from the mouths of babes–if we listen very carefully–we will hear the primordial words of our faith.

The earliest words are always the most important, and so it begins with the joyful "Ababababababa" for hours on end while rolling across the living room floor. In the exercising of the tongue, the most intimate name for God that we have known in human history, the one which we waited centuries for–to the insult of the dignified–naturally rolls off the lips of the five month old.

And it is only a matter of time–and a few consonants–until we hear "allelelele" over and over again. From God's name to God's praise. Are these words created by us? Or are we created for these words? Have we chosen them to address God, or have they chosen us? So close to our hearts, so close to our origins, are these words that it seems predestined that in our mastery of human language we should need to utter them.

Alleluia, the primordial expression of praise. The first prayer of all of us.

Today, as we prepare to enter into the season of Lent, we take pause to lift up this precious word, "Alleluia." For, during Lent, it is taken from us. Our first joy, our first prayer is taken from us.

To be buried like a seed. Not as a punishment–though it may feel like that–but so that in abstinence, our heart may remember our fondness, our natural inclination for the word that springs from our innermost being and rolls from our lips. We bury it like a seed so that it might grow. So that the spirit of praise will take root again in our lives and blossom with the Spring.

We bury it like a seed so that at the crack of dawn six weeks from now, we will recognize it once again as the *first* song of an Easter people.

2. *Aquinas Midday Prayer*
January 15, 2001
Matthew 4:13-17

Last Sunday we celebrated the Baptism of the Lord. The feast seems to serve as a bridge between the Christmas season that we are wrapping up and the Ordinary Time that we are beginning. In thinking about this over the past week, I began to reflect that the feast as much points us forward to what is coming as it point back to the season from which it came–and that continued meditation on its gospel might be a good thing at the beginning of this new semester.

Meeting Jesus in the infancy narratives that we have heard during the Christmas season presents us with a great paradox. He is born an ordinary baby, and yet angels announce his birth. He is laid in a manger amidst beasts of burden, yet the stars of the sky cradle him with light. He is found amidst lowly shepherds, yet kings bring him gifts. His parents are so poor they bring only turtle doves to his consecration in the temple, but they are welcomed by prophets.

They give him a most common name: *Jesus.*
But, in the readings of the last several weeks, we've heard him called:
> Ruler of the House of Jacob
> Heir of the Throne of David
> Emmanuel
> Messiah and Lord
> The Word Made Flesh
> The Light of the Gentiles
> The Glory of Israel
> Prince
> Shepherd of God's People

Now, today, we hear one last name. One last key to unlocking this man's identity. We have heard who he is to us. Now, we hear who he is to God.

He is *Beloved.* He is *Son.*

Names are an interesting thing. It is always an interesting conversation to debate the power of a name. We always say that we are not the same as our names. That what people call us doesn't really matter. But, would my life be radically different, if–from birth–my parents had named me Colleen (as my dad had advocated) instead of Ann? Or if they had named me Muffy or Zoe? All are fine names, but would I have become someone different than I am? Perhaps. We certainly continue to become more aware of the effects of name-*calling* on the self-esteem of children. How the label "Stupid" can haunt a person long after it is last applied. Names do shape us in a mysterious way as we become what we are called.

Many of the names attributed to Jesus in the infancy narratives we have focused on so prominently in the last few weeks, we know, were probably applied to him after he had died and rose. These infancy narratives were the last parts of the Gospels written–the fruit of much reflection by various disciples about the true identity of this man in their midst. They were applied by others to describe the Jesus they had experienced. Our Gospel today, however, gives us insight into how Jesus possibly experienced himself as named.

The event of Jesus' baptism by John is one of only a handful of stories that all four of the Gospels have in common. While each Gospel tells it slightly differently, by its frequency, we must be convinced of its powerful and formative effect on Jesus' life. Matthew and Mark lead us to believe that Jesus himself was the source of the story. For it is only Jesus who sees the sky rent in two and the Spirit descending like a dove. And, in the Gospel of Mark (the earliest of the Christian Gospels), it is only Jesus who hears the voice: "You are my beloved Son. On you my favor rests." While the Christian community would come to affirm this divine naming, we might guess that it began as Jesus' own spiritual insight that he shared with those closest to him.

Of all the names we have heard given to Jesus over the last couple weeks, this alone seems to be the one he heard himself. That one that whispered and boomed and echoed throughout his entire life. The one that shaped his whole person. The one that formed him into who he would become. "You are my beloved son."

Would Jesus have been Jesus without this name? Without this knowledge? We can speculate "no." The infancy narratives reveal several "epiphany" events in which Christ's true identity was made known to others. The story of Christ's baptism seems to reveal the

"epiphany" event in which Jesus' true identity became known to himself:
"I am the beloved son of God."

We can imagine how this knowledge must have made him feel—the joy,
the kind of tickle in the gut when one knows that one is the object of
infatuation, of affection. We can imagine how the world looked more
beautiful to Jesus—how the sun shone brighter, how the birds sang more
sweetly, how the flowers bloomed more radiantly—on the morning after
his baptism. "I am beloved." We can imagine how people became
friendlier, power figures less intimidating, hardship less frightening. "I
am beloved."

Jesus' baptism shaped his whole world view. It affected everything: the
work he would take on, the way he interacted with people, what he
preached, and eventually the way he would die. The knowledge of his
"beloved-ness," his "son-ship," gave him the courage and the conviction
to pick up the cross. Kept him faithful to the end. *This* was the man—
the beloved one—that God raised from the dead.

And *Beloved* is the name, above all other names, which led to us calling
upon him by *so many names.*

It is not his name alone, however. For, in Baptism, each one of us was
called "Beloved" by God. Each one of us was called "Child." For each
one of us the sky is rent and the Spirit descends. But have you heard
yet? You have come out of the water, but have you heard? Do you have
a tickle in your gut knowing that the Divine smiles down on you with
affection? Delights in your very being? Do you *really* know?

And are you letting this love form you? Is it shaping the way that you
look at the world? Is it determining your every activity, your every
interaction?

Is it giving you courage?
Is it giving you hope?
And, is it giving you strength to pick up that cross, to stare death in the
eye, and to know that God's faithfulness is always vindicated in
resurrection?

When we speak about the change of liturgical colors with the children
in the atrium, we speak about green as the "growing time" that follows
the "festal" white time. It is the time in which we let the "joy of the

feast grow in our hearts." As we enter into "green time" this week, it seems particularly fitting to continue to revel in this last great epiphany of the season of epiphanies. As we begin this new semester, before we drown in the demands about to be set upon us, let us share a few moments of silence this week to allow God look at us with affection, as on the day of our Baptism, and to hear the name that shapes us, the name that most "becomes" us, the name that gives reason for everything we are about to do.

3. *Aquinas Midday Prayer*
Black History Month Celebration
February 20, 2001
1 John 1: 1-5

A week and a half ago, I participated in one of several obligatory annual rituals on the Mees calendar: the OLS Pro-Life Square Dance. As organizer of the event, my mother desires a strong family & friend presence, though in retrospect, I must say that only my sister and I ever seem to respond to this most subtle pressure. My other siblings have found tactful means of excusing themselves from the four hour reverie, and even my husband has had mysterious, irreconcilable scheduling conflicts for the past two years. Funny how that one-weekend-per-year youth group retreat continues to coincide with the OLS Pro-Life Square Dance. Brendan Curran graciously filled in for a second time this year. But, beware, Brendan will be moving at the end of this May and none of you is safe when next February rolls around.

Among the neophytes in our 2001 dancing squares was a couple I had never met before, but who ended up being parents of a former highschool classmate. The man was eager to share the success of his daughter in college and her career. He was curious to know what I'd been up to... where I'd gone to college. "Kalamazoo." "Why?" he wanted to know. "Well, I'd always dreamed of going to Africa and Kalamazoo had the best undergrad African studies program in the country."

What followed was a string of the most blatant and ignorant remarks on race I think have ever been addressed for my ears to hear. When I say ignorant, I mean really—in the original sense of the word—ignorant. I don't say it as a judgment so much as a factual statement that he clearly had no knowledge, even book knowledge, of African or African-American history and culture.

At the end, he wanted to know: What good had it done to end up with a degree in African—and, little did he know, Russian—history? Of what use was that here? How was it at all helpful to me in my job now?

The tone was crude but the question legitimate. And, I think it has some parallels in the larger dialogue concerning February as black

7

history month. What really is the value of studying history–especially a history other than our own? It's not a particularly religious question, but it is one to which Christian tradition can and has to speak. Furthermore, it is a question undergirded by certain theological assumptions that should–and I have no doubt do–concern us as theologians. Number one on this list would be an unconscious re-scripting of verse 5 of the 1st letter of John embedded in many American minds that "God is white. In him there is no darkness at all."

Strange to say, the real theological problem with this rewrite isn't the first part. Every culture that I am aware of has drawn the map of the world with their land at the center; believes that the first man and woman came from their ethnic group; and originally visualized divinity as looking much like themselves. This is not inherently evil. In fact, I think we could say that it is very akin to the Christian understanding of an incarnational spirituality.

For a people to paint God in their image can be a reflection of a deep understanding that they are chosen and beloved by the divine, so beloved that God chooses to dwell in their midst, to share their lives. It can be a way of being faithful to their lived experience of a God who does not shun the material world but actively engages it. This is an understanding of God that Christianity affirms. To paint God white is testimony to our belief in Incarnation.

No, the real problem with the rewrite of 1st John 1:5 is what this new first half implies for the second half: "In God there is no darkness at all." We somehow think that God choosing and loving us so much means that God couldn't love and choose any other people like us–and that God's active presence in our history means God was never active anywhere else at any other time. *Our* history is salvation history; theirs isn't. So that in God, there is no otherness, no darkness, nothing that is not white.

Such an attitude implies that we possess the fullness of all there is to know in human experience of God. If so, we have no need to hear the testimony of others, no need to know of their experience, their history of interacting with the divine, because we have all that we need in our own. We already have the answers. We already know who God is. We can tell you, but we don't have anything to hear.

A truly Christian incarnational spirituality has to be one of paradox. It recognizes that where God dwells is the center of the universe and that this center is everywhere. That God is white *and* in God there is plenty of darkness. That God is black *and* in God there is plenty of whiteness.

To paint God a particular race is a dangerous thing if it is an end in itself. For Christians, inculturation is not the end; it is the pathway through which we move toward the Transcendent God who is beyond all color, beyond all knowing. In the oft-quoted words of Athanasius, "God became human so that humans might become gods." Christ's incarnation as one of us was to bring us beyond ourselves.

All healthy Christianity is inculturated Christianity. But inculturated Christianity only remains healthy when it realizes that it is inculturated. And this happens only when it is in conversation with other inculturated Christian communities—and even non-Christian ones.

The verses preceding 1 John 1:5 need to be read in this light for us to truly grasp the beauty and wisdom of the real verse 5. Often as we read these first four verses, we identify with the writer—or community of the writer—who does the proclaiming of their experience:
> "This is what we have heard and seen and touched with our
> very own bodies."
And it is good that we identify here. For we know that we are called to share the Good News of God in our midst.

But are we also able to envision ourselves in the position of the community who received such an epistle? Are we also a community that can—with awe and wonder—listen to the Good News as others have heard and seen and touched it in their bodies, in their life experience?

In their pastoral on evangelization, the Black bishops of the U.S. remind the church of what it gains in this listening to the many histories / cultures of which it is comprised. They write:

"There is a richness in our black experience that we must share with the entire people of God. These are gifts that are part of an African past. For we have heard with black ears and we have seen with black eyes and we have understood with an African heart. We thank God for the gifts of our Catholic faith, and we give thanks for the gifts of our blackness. In all humility we turn to the whole Church, that it might share our gifts so that 'our joy may be complete.'"

4. Aquinas Midday Prayer
April 17, 2001
John 20:11-18

Growing up, I always heard the stories of the empty tomb as stories of the resurrection. I had the impression that the disciples of Jesus went to the tomb, found it empty and jumped for joy. I had the impression that they immediately knew he had come back to life and ran off to tell everyone else. For the next forty days, Jesus played a great game of hide-and-go-seek with them. It was tremendous fun. And then, he moved on to heaven, but they continued to bask in the glow of the great trick they had played on the laws of nature. They were happy ever after. Yes, this is what I had thought: Jesus' tomb has been found empty, let the party begin.

Of course, none of the Gospels says this. They seem to indicate that exuberance was in short supply at the discovery of the empty tomb. None more so than the Gospel of John: The Beloved Disciple willing to believe, but not understanding; Peter simply returning home; Mary Magdelene staying behind—weeping. It behooves us to remember that before Easter morning was the bedrock of the Church's joy, it was the source of the disciples' horror.

I do not think that I understood that before this year.

As most of you know, my husband and I lost a baby last fall. Somewhere between weeks eight and ten, the little one's heart stopped beating. It had died before it had ever really begun to live, before we had ever even been able to settle on a name. Its due date was set for around my grandmother's birthday, and I had thought—if it were a girl— that we might name the baby after her. Our five year old was sure it would be called "Anakin Skywalker" or "Leopard Boy." But, after the silent ultrasound, the medical establishment, which couldn't seem to distinguish between the potential for human life and a tumor, began to give it different names—fetal matter, aberrant-cell-formation … which-should-be-removed. And so it was.

There are many sad things about having a miscarriage. But strangely, the worst part of it was waking up from an anesthesia I'd asked not to have and wondering what they had done with the tiny little remains of a

10

being I had begun to call child. I am not a meek or powerless woman. I can wield words quite well. But there was something about the sterile coldness of the hospital setting that made my emotions feel foolish and irrelevant. I couldn't find the courage to vocalize the strongest desire of my heart at the moment: to be able to give what would have been my child a "proper burial"–a place in the ground where I could occasionally visit and remember and once and a while place a flower. I was haunted by the idea of this baby being treated as medical waste–lying alone, without any acknowledgment of its humanity. Tombs are very important. And, when the tomb is empty, there is no place to localize the grief in one's life... and so it begins to restlessly pervade every space.

Motherhood is like a huge secret club. At each stage of a child's development, women come out of the woodwork to tell you all you ever wanted to know of their own stories, sometimes a little more. In my first pregnancy, I was initiated into every conceivable facet of childbearing. In my second pregnancy, I was initiated into every conceivable facet of child-losing. I was wrapped in the sorrow of all the mothers of the world who had lost their children, and, worse, don't know where to find them. I do not know whether it is good pastoral care to drown a sad person in stories of much greater sadness, but to the degree that it has increased my capacity for empathy, it is a good thing.

One begins to taste inklings of the agony of the mothers of the Plazo de Mayo in Latin America. The grandmothers of the disappeared in South Africa & Rwanda. The widowed of Bosnia. Women who weep over loved ones whose discarding was preceded by acts of great cruelty, of torture, of war. There are a hell of a lot of empty tombs in this world and never are they the cause of rejoicing. There are a hell of a lot of Mary Magdalenes weeping and wondering and searching for the vanished in this world and none of their stories has a happy ending.

Save one.

It is a little hard to know what to do with that one. For, on one level, as soon as the Risen Christ makes an appearance the parallel ends. We find that Mary's assumptions were ungrounded. It was not the gardener or the soldier or the Shining Path who snatched Jesus' body from the tomb. It was God.

We can resonate with her weeping and wondering. We can even stir our courage to demand his body. We know the strength of our intent would compensate for the weakness of our physique. That in love we, too, would personally carry our beloved back–from any distance or any location necessary–to the dignity of the tomb.

But, can we resonate with the remainder of the story? Does the empty tomb of a resurrected Jesus have anything to say to the empty tombs of our world?

I think perhaps two things.

First, it invites us to a new relationship to the empty tomb as a place of potential for God to act. The empty tomb becomes an image of the Last Day. Jesus' body was the first snatched from the tomb by God, but only the first. A symbol of hope for what will happen to all of us and our loved ones at the close of time, wherever they may be and whenever this might happen. The snatching of Jesus was the beginning of the end time. Hence our stance before the empty tomb is no longer one of complete despair, but of waiting. Not waiting for the sin of the world to return the dead and fill the grave. Not waiting for an old relationship to be restored or brought to "closure." But, a waiting on the faithfulness of God to "do a new thing"… to recreate possibilities for relationship that do not un-do death, but are not obstructed by it either. It is the place of potential for a new kind of relationship.

This being so, we can also say that the empty tomb of Jesus initiates us to a way of waiting for the Last Day… a way of waiting for the fullness of new relationship. It is a way of living with absence. The discovery of Jesus' on-going presence with them–beyond the grave–was surely a great joy for the disciples. But at the same time, this resurrected-presence-stuff is rough to live with.

The "forty days" of mysterious appearances were not a re-living of old times, where they would kick back and talk about the weather and the lilies of the field. They were a boot camp in the discipleship of waiting. An intense training in how to recognize Jesus' presence–Jesus' Spirit–when their eyes could not see him. Eyes are not to be trusted any more in discerning the divine touch. Rather, Mary will come to recognize him in the Word, in the hearing of her name being spoken. The disciples of Emmaus will come to recognize him in the breaking of the bread. Thomas will come to recognize him in the touch of wounds.

As the Johannine community continued to meditate on their experience, they would come to recognize him in light, in water, in wine overflowing. Perhaps it was only when their imagination was expanded in this way could they begin to recognize his presence also in the Pharisee Paul, in the Gentile Cornelius, in those persons and nations where they might have least expected it.

The Church shows us that the way to live with absence is to live sacramentally. To live with antenna up and heart ready for sudden breakthroughs between heaven and earth.
This is the way we wait for the Parousia.
This is the way we live in a communion of saints—some of whom are living and some of whom are dead and some of whom are missing.
This is how we live in faith before—in fact—every sort of tomb.

The empty tomb stories are not stories of resurrection but stories of learning live with resurrection. This means that if we were to celebrate this Easter in the spirit of the first disciples, it should probably be about 10 % balloons and banner waving and about 90% staring out the window with our jaws dropped, pondering.

How long did it take for their party to begin?

How long did it take for this huge gaping, empty hole in the side of a cliff to reconcile with its counterpart in their hearts?

How long did it take to learn to say, "I have seen the Lord" when one has not literally *seen* anything that looked like the Lord at all?

I suspect Easter was not so much an event as a process. A process in which the joyful knowledge of Jesus' resurrection watered by the tears of longing slowly grew a certain kind of hope—rich in the power to heal and make wise, strong in the capacity to endure.

This is the kind of tenacious hope that grows out of cracks in the sidewalk and alley. Whose roots will not surrender to the floods. Whose leaves will not wither with frost. This is the kind of hope that Churches can be built upon.

Let us pray this Easter season—our fifty days of "processing"—for this hardiest of hopes to grow again in our hearts and in the hearts of all the Magdalenes throughout the earth.

5. *Aquinas Midday Prayer*
Rosh Hashana
September 18, 2001
Luke 12: 51-53

(This preaching was given one week after 9-11.)

It's Jesus' fault, really,
Suggests French literary scholar, Rene Girard.
Because, we had it all worked out, you see.
Whenever people are together, there is conflict.
And, if we are to survive, it must be remedied.

We found a way to do it.
A crisp, almost mathematical formula,
Tried and true:
Everyone minus one.

If you want peace in your community,
If you want to stop the chaos,
Identify one person, one group, one nation
And have everyone focus their gaze there.
Look closely.
See how they are not quite like any other.
See how they have clearly caused this disruption.
See how the whole group suffers because of them.
And listen to the whisper of Caiaphas:
I mean, really, even if it weren't *entirely* their fault,
Would it not be better to excise one than have all civilization crumble?

And, when the one dies and the riot is quelled,
Are we not grateful?
Do we not experience unity?
Must this not be a divinely-sanctioned exercise
If it produces such peace among us?
Could we not say that this limited violence was a good... even holy activity?
Does God not only bless, but demand the sacrifice?

14

The silent scapegoat has taken our anger away
Has rid us of our fury.
We always knew there was something special about this one.
Didn't we?
Even something god-like.

And, if we build them a tomb,
We can keep our focus fixed there, for a very long time.
And, our peace will be extended.

And, we can write a glorious story of the One-sent-from-on-high,
The One-born-to-die-so-that-we-might-have-life.
And, so long as we could tell the myth and call the violence sacred
We could remain in peace.

It's Jesus' fault, really.
We had thousands of years of beautiful stories.
Thousands of words for hiding our murders.
And in not one of them did the victim speak.
In not one of them did we hear the tale from the victim's point of view.
It seemed like such a fool-proof system.
Until he struck at its Achilles.

For his voice would not be silenced by death.
The tomb would not keep hold of his body.
No myth would overwrite the violence done to him.
No burial site would mesmerize and bind his followers.
For the first time in human history, the story was told from another
point of view:
The victim of violence spoke.
The voice hidden by myth was uncovered in gospel.
A veil torn in two.
We could see.
And, we did not feel dispassionate admiration.
And, we did not feel peaceful and tamed and united.
Stirring in our hearts was a new emotion for the victim:
We felt empathy.

It's all Jesus fault, really.
For in him we first heard the voice of the One subtracted from
Everyone
And our system began to crumble.

For those who have heard and felt the pain of the victim can no longer find peace in his death.
Their rituals become ineffective.
Their myths no longer hide.
Their mathematical systems for keeping order fail.

We keep trying to run the program.
Over and over again we type in:
Everyone minus one. Everyone minus one.
But there is a virus in our system.
"ERROR" flashes across the screen with one of those horrid images of a tiny, lit bomb.
Our program for peace has been destroyed.

It's Jesus fault, really
That now the word "victim" stirs pity.
That now the status—which in ancient times, no one wanted—
Now everyone clamors for.
That what once implied silence, now gains the platform from which to speak.
And as the virus continues to spread
And our methods for peace continue to flail
The violence continues to grow—an estimated 110 million dead in the past century alone.

It's all Jesus' fault, really
That we are stuck in a horrible, horrible time.
For in his death and resurrection, he has destroyed our old way of being.
And, if we continue to try and make it work…
If we continue to believe that killing a few Americans or Afghanis or Irish or Israelis
or Palestinians or Pakistanis
will somehow bring us peace…
If we continue to hope that we will be able to just patch up a system with a fatal flaw and all will return to how it was before…
We will self-destruct.

The Jesus-virus doesn't allow us to make amendments in our current way of doing things.
It forces us to re-write the entire program.
To find a way to create peace with Everyone.

Just Everyone.
No minuses allowed.

It's our decision, really
Between death and the abandonment of all we have known.
Between the lovely subtleness of myth and the blinding light of truth.

It's our decision, really
Though I doubt we can do it on our own.
For we are a people who struggle tremendously to even stop smoking
Who can't uphold resolutions to avoid chocolate
Who spend years in therapy to break out of a single dysfunctional
family pattern.
How will *we* ever, *ever* change the foundations upon which human
civilization is built?
What could *we* ever, *ever* do to escape the gravitational weight of
original sin?

There can be no formula for peace for Everyone.
The only alternative to Everyone minus One
Is Everyone plus One.

It's our decision, really
How we will tell this story.
Will we speak of re-building, revenging, re-investing in the patterns of
Old Adam, searching out isolated vignettes of hope?
Or will we simply admit that there is no hope for us save falling on our
knees before the New Adam and begging him to show us another way
of being human?
This day begins the first day of Rosh Hashana.
The first day of the new year on the Jewish calendar.
It marks the anniversary of the day, not when the world was created
But when humankind was created.
It is the celebration of Adam.
For, in Jewish thought, it was only in the creation of the human person
—who could assent in free will—
that God became Sovereign over the Universe.
And so the shofar is blown in memory of this eternal coronation.

Today is the day in which the Book of Life and the Book of Death are
unlocked.

The opening of a ten-day window during which our actions will have tremendous weight.

Ten days we have in which to make things right with our fellow humans.

A reconciliation which must precede the last day,
which is set aside to make things right with God.

These days—referred to as the Days of Awe—
will close at sunset on Yom Kippur.
On that evening, the name of each person
is permanently inscribed in one of the two books.
The tomes are sealed and the year is determined.
The window of opportunity for conversion will have passed.

Today is the day the Jewish people define as "a wake up call."
Have we not heard its alarm?
What shall we do in these Days of Awe ...
so numbered before our fates are sealed?
Who will reign over human kind?

It's our decision, really.

6. *Aquinas Midday Prayer*
November 20, 2001
2 Maccabees 6:18-31

The day of my great revelation began—quite literally—in HELL.

It began when I awoke from a night of restless, sweaty doses of sleep to find myself stuffed, with three other exchange students, in the backseat of a rusting taxi... still.

It began with the loud squawking of chickens and a vendor pounding on the dusty window, sliding plastic watches from China through the crack at the top of the pane.

It began on a day that did not feel like a new day, but rather the extension of the one before, which had been an extension of the week before it, and the month before that. For, it had been almost six weeks that we'd been stuffed inside one taxi or another.

We'd left Sierra Leone when the army shut down our college bearing tear gas and guns. When rumors of a coup were in the air.

We thought things might be better elsewhere in West Africa. But after being held against our will by a drugged man in Senegal, relieved of much of our money and a passport in Mali, and narrowly escaping imprisonment in Guinea, Sierra Leone was looking pretty good again... and we thought we'd head back there.

It began in yet another taxi park.
Where the driver of our cab was sure he could find one more person
to jam into the car.
One more person on a circular journey from bad to what looked better, but usually turned out worse.

It began when I finally raised my drooping eyelids to look for some sign of where we were in time and space.
"6:10 a.m." read the plastic watch dangling next to my head.
"HELL" read the sign outside the window.
Somewhere around 6:15 a.m., I realized that we were next to a dilapidated petrol station from which the "S" had fallen from the front of

the company name. It did not stop me from nudging my traveling companion Ellen, however, and pointing out to her: "Hey, we finally made it."

But, of course, we hadn't.
Because when you think that the outlook cannot grow any bleaker…
it can.
Around 11 a.m. on the-day-that-began-in-hell,
The taxi hissed, banged, and came to a sudden halt.
All of us on-the-journey-from-bad-to-what-looked-better realized this definitely looked worse.

The driver popped the hood and started futzing around with whatever demons reside under there. I stood out on the dirt road, in the middle of a dense jungle and looked—in both directions—as far as the eye could see… for another sign of human life.

In the four hours or so since leaving the taxi park, we had not passed another car going in either direction. It could be *hours*…. It could be *days* before anyone found us. And, what if it were one of those days that stretched into a week into a month?

My mind began to run wild.

None of our parents had any idea where in the world we were.
Would the college in Sierra Leone even notice we were missing?
Does the U.S. embassy come looking for people after a couple of months?

And then, like a bolt of Pauline lightning, it came to me:
A revelation so simple that to say it out loud seems ridiculous
were it not so true.
One of two things is going to happen, I realized:

Either I am going to live through this… or I am going to die.
And, if I believe in resurrection, well, it doesn't make a whole lot of difference.

In a moment, something that I had always known theoretically
—at least in my head—
was understood in my heart
And the world began to spin.

Either I am going to live through this… or I am going to die.
And, if I believe in resurrection… all is *still* well.

Quite suddenly the road was not a road, but a clearing in the jungle that didn't necessarily go anywhere but *here*.
And *here* was so strangely beautiful.

Sometimes mystics on the cusp of surrender see visions of other worlds.
But, in that moment, I saw a vision of this one.
There were trees great and varied in a hundred shades of green.
And insects with transparent wings veined in gold.
Birds with cobalt heads sang songs sweeter than caramel.
The trill of an unusual frog rang like a telephone.
And intertwined vines formed Jacob's ladder
rising into the hazy gray sky.
It would seem hell and heaven are not separated by a great chasm after all, but by a country so narrow that one can begin the day in one realm and make it for lunch in the other, traveling at only 25 miles an hour.

Either I am going to live through this… or I am going to die.
And, if I believe in resurrection… all is still well.

It was a personal revelation that utterly changed my life, but I was not the first to have it, nor the first to be radically affected by it. That privilege belonged to the Jews of the second century BCE, and its impact is first testified to in our readings this week, particularly Eleazar's testimony today and the Jewish mother with seven sons tomorrow.

For the hundreds of years prior to the events of Maccabees, the Jewish people had not believed in a continuation of life after death.
Either they lived through it … or they died… and it made a great deal of difference.

Theirs was a God that hated death and actively staved it off:
A God who held back the hand poised to sacrifice Isaac.
Who ended their slavery in Egypt
Who rescued them from starvation in the desert.
But theirs was a God who didn't seem to say much about what happened when death did occur.

Theirs was a god of the living and was uninvolved with the dead.
Death remained a mystery.
Because they understood the human person as an *animated body* rather than an *incarnated spirit,*
they could not imagine an un-embodied existence.
One might live in memory, so long as descendants existed.
But, otherwise, there was only *Sheol*–
> the antithesis of life,
> the shadowy void of nothingness.

At the same time, though, theirs was a God of Justice–a God who set things right. And, ever so slowly, the ramifications of this conviction began to transform Jewish thought on death.

If God were a God of Justice, then death must be the just punishment for the peoples' sin.
But sometimes… sometimes there were persons who were righteous… and they *still* suffered and they *still* died.
And where was the justice in that?

The day of their great revelation began on a journey from Babylonian exile to what looked better, but only turned out worse.
They'd repented from their sin, reorganized their society, rebuilt their temple–but still did not know freedom.

It began when their temple was consecrated to a foreign god, when the diet they held as sacred was demeaned.
It began when the Law of Life became the source of their deaths.
It began when their experience engaged in a dual with their doctrine.

The easiest answer would have been to let go of their conviction in God's justice. For many cultures viewed their gods as arbitrary, viewed life as hopelessly unfair. But, the Jews did not let go.

Rather they believed the more difficult:
That even in misery, when things seem irreparably unjust,
when even the righteous die,
There must be something more to God's justice
A justice that extends beyond death –
A way that God redeems even the dead
A life beyond what we can see
And in the end, all will still be set right…. All is still well.

This is the conviction of Eleazar and the Jewish mother. This is the hope of Maccabees.

It has proved to be a dangerous hope.
When–in time–the final justice of God became too separated from this world, it often produced a passivity in which people would accept their current oppression because it would be remedied in the world to come.
When–in time–the description of God's final justice took on the details of a paradise, it inspired suicidal bravado, even fundamentalist terrorism.

But, while it made some foolish, it kept many faithful.
At the juncture of time and eternity, it gave the ability to live freely,
>to choose rightly,
>to see clearly,
>to cling loosely,
>to confront crisis without fear.

And gave to our tradition its very first martyrs–including Eleazor, the Jewish mother, and her seven sons. For before we believed in resurrection, history gives us no evidence of the courage needed to stare death in the eye and still choose it.

We mark among this number our very own Lord, who–in contrast to the Sadduccees of his day–took the "Maccabee-an revelation" as his own and walked, in full freedom toward Jerusalem,
>–A pilgrim on the journey toward what looked-better-but-would-likely-turn-out-worse–

Recognizing that
>Either he was going to live through this,
>or he was going to die,
>But that–even if it were the latter–
>God's justice would prevail.

And, he saw all would be well

And, he saw the grass of the field,
And, he saw the lilies clothed like Solomon-in-glory
And, he saw the blue-black feathers of the raven.
To the caramel songs of sparrows,
He saw a valley of darkness with a hundred shades of green.

7. *Aquinas Midday Prayer*
April 9, 2002
Acts 4:32–5:11

(This preaching took place during the height of the sex abuse scandal in the Catholic Church.)

Late in the seventeenth century a great debate arose among the learned of the West regarding the location of the Garden of Eden.

Antonio de Leon Pinelo argued for Brazil. Grounded in the allusion of Tertullian to an equatorial location for the earthly paradise, Pinelo persuasively asserted that *surely* the four rivers springing from one sacred land referred to the Rio de la Plata, the Amazon, the Orinoco, and the Magdelena.

The Dominican Luis de Urreta agreed an equatorial garden was most likely–but in Africa, not South America. De Urreta suggested Mount Amara in Ethiopia. "Amara" means "paradise" in the local language–a divine hint further reinforced by the lovely flowers and year-round temperate climate this mount enjoys because of its higher altitude.

By the early eighteenth century, the equatorial bias gave way to theories focusing on Armenia, Mesopotamia, and Palestine. The present location of the Tigris and Euphrates Rivers lent themselves to support this proposition–even if the Pishon and Gihon had disappeared without a trace.

Although it was well established that the flood of Noah might have erased all historical remains of the garden, a latent hope persisted: if we read scripture seriously enough and hunted persistently enough, we just might stumble upon the "cherubim" and the "fiery revolving sword." We just might knock at the gate that locked our ancestors out, and somehow be readmitted.

As modern Catholics influenced by decades of historical criticism, we find these quests rather amusing. Though occasionally tantalized by the History Channel special (using new NASA satellite photos of ancient dry river beds in Turkey) we've given up hope for locating that elusive garden of the East.

Eden has become for us a literary tool–part of a larger story about the nature of human experience wracked with disappointment and suffering. In the face of evil, the symbol of Eden allows us to hold onto the conviction that God's original intent for us was good. God's desire was for a harmonious and obedient community enjoying the abundance of God's generosity and affection.

But, we recognize that Eden does not exist on its own; it never did. It exists only in the context of the Fall. There is no idyllic world removed from this one, free of competition and envy and dishonesty. Neither scouring history nor the back roads of the Middle East will uncover one. Eden is not a separate place unto itself. Eden, we recognize, is none other than the foundational subtext–the latent hope–of our current world, pocked as it is with sin.

The funny thing is that, at the same period of my life in which I delighted in popping the fundamentalist bubble around Eden, I was downright driven in my quest for the Church of Acts, chapter 4–the New Testament Eden described by Luke in today's first reading. I remember having a passionate conversation with a priest-friend about the opulence of the contemporary Church: the scandal of the gilded ceiling while there were poor in the streets, the staleness of the liturgy, the politics and back-stabbing within the congregation. The Church of Acts was an entirely different thing. It was white; we were scarlet. But, this Church could be recovered if we scoured the genesis of our *ekklesia* for indications of how to find the original and ideal Pentecost creation. We could yet discover how to pass by the blazing sword that kept us from our truest selves. I hunted for the Church of Acts like de Urreta pursued Eden.

Imagine how disappointed I was to find the fossils of Paul. To realize that even in the earliest of the epistles, written years before Acts, the Church was already struggling, already experiencing a dichotomy between its rich and poor members, already losing people who fell out of windows during rambling preaching, already polarized by its leaders. The Church of Acts 4, it turns out, never existed on its own, but only as part of a larger story, for which we must read the opening of Acts 5.

We do not hear much of Ananais and Sapphira. While all of us know the story of Adam and Eve, their New Testament counterparts have received little attention. But, we can imagine how they first came to find their place in scripture:

Like ourselves, the believers of Luke's community had heard the Good News of the Risen Christ.
Had heard of the defeat of Satan.
Had come to believe in the washing away of sin at Baptism.
The washing away of sin's penalty–death. They had come to know of the outpouring of Jesus' own Spirit.

But what difference had it made?
How was it that all this could be true–
       when still they suffered,
       and still their members died,
       and still disharmony persisted?
How do we explain the presence of evil in a community of the baptized?
Is it not a scandal to the very essence of the Christian proclamation?

Luke's answer to the presence of evil within the Church was to restructure Genesis' answer to the presence of evil in the world. He reconfirms that God's intention for us was only good: God's desire was for a harmonious and obedient community enjoying the abundance of God's generosity and affection.

But even in the community of the New Adam, even when the slate has been wiped clean in the Blood of the Lamb, the freedom of the human person still exists... and even the most *venial* of selfish choices can have the most *profound* of effects.

With the small withholding of a percentage of profit from the sale of a property, sin enters into the sparkling new Easter community of believers for the first time.

It seems so minor–not unlike the sneaking of a piece of fruit–hardly capable of explaining the cataclysmic train wreck that describes the state of the Church today. And Luke's introduction of the sin of Ananais and Sapphira may not satisfy our curiosity (much less our anguish) about how the Church of Acts 4 became the Church that molests adolescents, any more than the story of Adam and Eve adequately explains the current war in Israel or AIDS in Africa. It is never easy to understand evil, for the abundance of chaos it reaps is always so much greater than the sum total of individual human choices. The whole is greater than its parts. And perhaps no story could do.

But, the reading of this day does offer us a challenge in the midst of our Easter joy. Lest our eschatological celebration become too detached from the reality of this world, it asks us who are baptized how total our conversion from sin has been.

How firmly did we shout out our answer to the renewal of our baptismal promise at the vigil: "Do you reject Satan and all his empty promises?"

Now, how thoroughly do we live it?

Do we give the whole-hearted witness of a Barnabas–or the half-hearted witness of Ananais and Sapphira?

Are we aware of the impact that our individual choices have on the whole of the community?

We shall never find the Church of Acts, chapter 4. But, perhaps we shall find small consolation in the fact that, literally speaking, we can't. It turns out that the word "Church" does not appear in the New Testament until the end of the Ananais and Sapphira episode.

The word we use to describe ourselves is not used until after we have known and acknowledged sin in our midst. Technically, there is no church before sin. There is no Eden separate from the fallen world.

There is only eternal hope that God is good, that God's will for us is only good, and that God's dreams for us will never die.

8. *Evening Prayer for Dominican Formation Community*
Feast of St. Catherine of Siena
April 29, 2002

(This preaching took place during the height of the sex abuse scandal in the Catholic Church.)

A Reading from the last letter of Catherine, to Raymond of Capua:

"The fire increased more and more in me and I had only one thought: what I could do to offer up myself to God for Holy Church and to deliver those whom God had given into my hands from ignorance and negligence. Then the devils shouted death upon me and would hinder and repress my desire which filled them with terror. And they struck hard at me, but my desire grew freer and stronger, and I cried: '*O, eternal God, accept my life as a sacrifice for the mystical body of Holy Church. I can give nothing but what Thou hast given me Thyself. Take the heart then. Take the heart and press out the blood of it over the face of the Bride.*

"Then God looked in mercy upon me and He tore out the heart and pressed it out over Holy Church. And He seized it with such force that if He had not at once girded me about with His strength–for he would not that the vessel of my body should be broken–I should have passed hence. Then the devils shrieked worse than before... But hell has no power against the strength of humility and the light of holy faith; I collected my thoughts the more and labored as though with glowing irons; before the face of God, I heard words so sweet and promises that filled me with joy. And because it was all so hidden my tongue is no longer able to speak....

"We shall conquer the devil, not by the suffering itself borne in our bodies, but by virtue of that fire which is divine and exceedingly ardent and inestimable love. *Deo gratias, Amen. Gesu dolce, Gesu amore.*"

Preaching:

As a child, I was deeply enchanted with the orange St. Joseph edition of *Catholic Saints for Boys and Girls.* There were several St. Catherines in this book and it was difficult to keep them all straight. The easiest one to distinguish was St. Catherine Laboure. She wore a most unusual hang-glider-like contraption on her head and looked as though she might be whipped away upon the next gust of wind. Second in line, however, was Catherine of Siena. She was fairly easy to spot because she was always carrying a large wooden ark on her shoulder. I wondered what that was all about: Growing up, I met many people who walked around with a "chip on their shoulder," but never anyone with a ship on their shoulder.

Until recently, I had assumed that the ship was an iconographers invention—a symbol of the role that Catherine had played in steering the Church through the rocky waters of the Avignon papacy. Only in rereading the story of Catherine's life this past week did I realize that the image of Catherine bearing the bark was not an artist's creation, but one deeply rooted in Catherine's own imagination—based on an event which took place shortly before her death, shortly before the letter we read tonight was written:

The early months of 1380 found Catherine in Rome, praying for the new pope Urban, hopeful that reform was eminent, worried that it was not. These months found Catherine daily in the original St. Peter's Basilica, before the tomb of the first apostle. They found Catherine fixated upon Giotto's mosaic of the apostle's humble fishing vessel—an image of *la Navicella.*

One Sunday during Vespers, her disciple Tommaso Caffarini testifies, "while the winter evening began to creep in over the city," Catherine watched the bark leave the mosaic and come to rest squarely on her shoulders. Her companions saw nothing, but witnessed the fragile, thin Catherine collapse to the ground as if crushed by its weight. She was paralyzed and had to be carried home. She never recovered, and three months later, she died.

There was a time when flying boats would have rubbed me the wrong way. There was a time when much of the Catherine of Siena story would have rubbed me the wrong way. And still, if Catherine were a field education student, it is unlikely she would pass. We'd have to have some conversations about the virtues of living a healthy balanced life, about dealing with guilt and grief, about psychosomatic manifestations. Catherine's ministry and its accompanying spirituality emerged out a cultural and historical context very different than our own, and our ideas about what constitutes a holy life style–about what constitutes the "human person fully alive"–have continued to shift over time.

And yet, for all our language about balance and health and care of self, chances are that when we reflect on the conclusion of Catherine's life and writings this April 29th, 2002, we are not rubbed wrongly, but rather sympathetically.

We know a little more this year about the weight of *la Navicella*.
We understand a little better this year what it means to carry that weight on one's shoulders.
We identify a little more this year with what it is like to be crushed by free-falling mosaics.
For some in society, the weight of *la Navicella* is something that they see in the newspaper on the shoulders of a painfully stooped pope.
For most in this room, though–among the ministerial caste of the Church–it is something not only witnessed from afar, but carried in the inner most recesses of the heart.
> A deep sadness.
> A gravest of worries.
> A blackest of fears.
> A crushing, almost paralyzing, weight.

And we know it'd be smarter to run
That no good can come from propping up with our own bodies a ship that seems so determined to sink.
That soon ministerial leadership will be ranked up there with smoking and race car driving as a life insurance risk.
But, against all our better judgment, we don't.
We can't.

Instead we find ourselves praying crazy things in the middle of the night, like–
> "Use me Lord.
> I offer my whole self on behalf of this Church.
> And, if I had a thousand lives,
> Every one of them would be given to this people.
> And, if I had a thousand magic wishes,
> Every one of them would be for their healing.
> Let me be of service however I can, even if it means I suffer.
> Take this heart, Lord, and pour it out over your Church."

As if we had the heart of Christ living inside us or something.
And maybe we do.

And maybe we realize that perhaps Catherine
was not so different after all.
Or perhaps we are crazier than we thought.

This is the craziness of love.
It's the craziness that allows marriages to last 50 plus years.
The craziness that allows parents to last through the teenage years.
The craziness that allows religious to celebrate diamond jubilee years.
The craziness that allows the Church to survive through 2000 years.

It's the craziness that perpetuates creation, that breathes life into the
dead, that hopes for a new day–every day.
This is the crazy, salvific love of God.

And it is a mystery to us.
It is a mystery how that which we love so much
might end up crushing us.
And how that which crushes us gives us life.
And it's hard to know when God's desire that we have abundant life
means we must go.
And when God's desire that *all* have abundant life means we must stay.

Perhaps Catherine is not the best of *models* in this decision.
After all, she died emaciated and tormented at the age of thirty-three.
This is not any thing that I would wish for any of us.
But, Catherine is perhaps the best of *companions* in this journey along
the tightrope of ecclesial life.
Someone who knows exactly our struggles to be faithful and truthful
and loving in this community, even if it kills us.
Someone who can empathize tenderly with the weight we carry, as we
stand in reverence of the weight she carried.
Of the many saintly Catherines we might befriend in our tradition–from
Alexandria to Bologna to Sweden–this frail yet fiery woman from Siena
is one to whom we should wish to draw near:
For she will teach us about the excruciating paradoxes of love… "divine
and exceedingly ardent, and inestimable love."

"Deo gratias, Amen. Gesu dolce, Gesu amore."

9. *Aquinas Midday Prayer*
November 12, 2002
Titus 2:1-8, 11-14

In the movie Dead Poet Society, there is a delicious scene that takes place at the beginning of the school year, when the new literature professor–played by Robin Williams–opens the course by having the students turn to page such and such and begin to read from their textbooks a definition of prose by Pritchard.

It is standard textbook stuff.

Within four lines the students are already nodding off. And then Williams stands up and says, "Now I want you to tear that page out of your book." Everyone wakes up quickly, but no one moves. "Tear it out," he encourages. The expressions on the students' faces betray a wide range of emotion: bewilderment, daring, fear, horror, excitement.

One student, in particular–the one who will emerge as the main character in the drama–is paralyzed by all of these emotions at once. *He* is torn and you can read it in his body language. "This is a text book. We don't destroy text books. On the other hand, this page does nothing for me. I've never ripped out a page before. That'd feel awfully good. But, this *is* a text book."

There's something about the look on that student's face that captures for me the tension I feel inside of myself when I come across passages that discuss proper behavior of women in the Pauline or pastoral epistles–including the passage from the Letter to Titus that is prescribed for us today.

I have a great respect for textbooks; and I have a *really, really* great respect for the Bible as a text. There is a certain integrity to our Bible as a whole that I want to preserve and honor. And, I am really glad that nobody ripped out this page before I got to see it. This passage from Titus is a wonderfully illuminating historical document. "Isn't this interesting?" a part of me says.

The first Christians had just had their imagination blown to bits. The Kingdom of God, Jesus had said, belonged not to the elite, but the poor.

Gentiles could enter it before Jews. Sinners before Pharisees. And now, the proclaimer of this Kingdom, who was dead, had been raised to life. Everything they had once known as reliable had been turned on its head. All was up for grabs.

Tomorrow the sun might rise at 2 a.m.,
one moon might suddenly become three,
Ezekiel's chariots might swoop down from the heavens and end time.
Anything was possible.

We were as close to a *tabula rasa* community as there ever will be,
as free as any humans since Adam and Eve to organize our households
anew... and...

And we still constructed our communities to look remarkably like the familiar family and political structures of the day. The code of behavior we choose to lift up for our young women is the same code of behavior espoused in contemporary Greco-Roman wedding rituals. Isn't that interesting?

The world as we know it ends, but we continue to live day to day life very much the same—"consistent with sound doctrine",
> a thinly-veiled plea for "common sense,"
> a thinly-veiled euphemism for "the obvious,"
> "what everyone knows is good and right,"
> *really* a thinly-veiled disguise for the particular imagination of
> the local culture.

When we try to figure out how we will hold and carry new revelation within ourselves, within our common life together, we discover the only wineskins we come equipped with are old.

As a chapter out of our tradition's past, this passage offers a privileged glimpse into the imagination of our ancestors in the faith—its expansiveness (for clearly there were some pretty culturally-revolutionary things going on in the name of Christ) but also its limitations, the blind spots that it didn't seem to be aware of. I am glad that the scriptures offer such glimpses into our past. I am glad to know that, even in our origins, we struggled with having imaginations that are inherently embedded in a cultural context; with the dilemma of how much to blend in with the society around us; with how to be both prudent and prophetic at the same time. I am glad that the Bible gives testimony to these struggles. It makes me feel consoled about our present ecclesial life.

But, then again, this passage is not only in the Bible. It's in our lectionary–that selection of scripture passages, approximately 13% of the Bible as a whole, that the Church chooses to consistently proclaim to shape the imagination of today's faithful. When scripture is lifted up in the context of liturgy, we are not reading it as an interesting piece of historical *description*. In Christian communities around the world this day, it will be heard–with few exceptions–as *prescription*. And lest we doubt that the constructors of the lectionary recognized that the readings *are* heard in that way, let us observe what has been excised from the middle of this particular lection: vs. 9-10–where the author instructs slaves to be "submissive to their masters, pleasing them in every way, not contradicting them nor stealing from them, but expressing a constant fidelity by their conduct."

For some reason, *this* is no longer acceptable to proclaim followed by the phrase "The Word of the Lord," but to encourage older women to participate in the "Uncle Tom-like" structure of telling younger women to "be busy at home, under the control of their husbands" *is*. Now, isn't *that* interesting?

Each of us here today have had our own imaginations shaped powerfully by the "canon within a canon" that is our lectionary. For myself, I suspect that this reading and others like it–including the passage regularly read on the Feast of the Holy Family–have had a particular influence on my imagination and my family's imagination, even if primarily subliminal.

It comes mostly in the form of a nagging doubt that I have stepped out of my proper place, that I should be more humble and respectful, that maybe its not possible to balance work and home life, that I do not give enough of myself to my family. And all of those might be true, but I haven't heard the male members of my family (who are excellent, holy human beings) struggle with such doubts in the same way.

It comes in the form of conversations that continue to linger in my mind six years after they've been had: a very loving, religious parent who admits, "Well, I want to support what you are doing, but really I think that you should be staying at home." Whereas yesterday someone could have told me they think I should get out there and preach more often, and I'd have already forgotten.

In my life, these scriptures have not been wielded like weapons, as they sometimes have for others. Their impact has been much more subtle, boxing in *my* imagination—*my* capacity to conceive of other ways of being a woman in this time after the resurrection,
> when the sun might suddenly rise at 2 a.m.,
> when one moon might suddenly become three,
> when Ezekiel's chariots could come squealing around the corner at any minute,
> the time when I *should* be living in the freedom of knowing once and for all that *nothing* is impossible for God.

And so here I stand with a great big beautiful new book in front of me and a fierce urge to tear. And an urge to preserve. And an excitement about what could be. And a fear. And a love of this sacred text. And a sadness.

And a prayer: That I, that you, that our church, might be gifted with an imagination worthy of holding and living the news of the resurrection.

10. Aquinas Midday Prayer
Feast of the Annunciation
March 25, 2003
Luke 1:26-38

The history of Israel begins with a woman named Sarah and her wandering husband Abraham who follow directions no one else hears– the commands of an unknown god with dubious powers, only promises. It begins with a triad of visitors in the heat of the day who speak with one voice, and make the most fantastic promise yet–a long-desired son unsealing the womb of the long-barren Sarah, her child-bearing years long-past. It begins with a hearty laugh, and a question (that sounds perhaps more like a dare): "Is *anything* impossible for the Lord?"

Is anything impossible for the Lord?

It is a question that ricochets throughout Israel's history.
Cresting on the waves of the Red Sea.
Whistling through the sand hills of the Sinai desert
coated with a thin crust of manna.
Thundering as the walls of Jericho tumbled and fire rained down
on the drenched offering of Elijah
Hummed in the lullabyes of Hannah
Shouted with glee as Goliath's body hit the ground with a thud…
And Judith returned with the dripping head of Holofernes.

Is anything impossible for the Lord?

Cyrus, the mysterious Persian, emerges from nowhere
to end an endless exile.
Lamps with oil for one night remain lit for eight.
Water spurts from rocks.
Donkeys talk.
Men sleep with lions and sing in furnaces
To the echoing refrain of Miriam's tamborine

Is anything impossible for the Lord?

In the course of *time*, Israel saw its unknown God of Promises step out of the shadows to respond to Sarah's dare–slowly moving from unknown toward known, from promise toward action, from un-carnate toward incarnate.

Month by month,
year by year,
century by century,
everyday life punctuated rhythmically
by a series of most unlikely events–
A melody line unfolding, though sometimes lost amidst the other cacophonous patterns of history, equally intricate.
Crescendo-ing unto the heat of that day in the tiny village of Nazareth, when to Sarah's most distant daughter was given–once and for all– heaven's definitive answer:
A great resounding, "NO!" from the mouth of Gabriel,
"No. *Nothing* is impossible with God."

And, you, Mary, shall carry within you God's final answer–given in the form of a child, whose whole existence will be a paradox, an impossibility from the beginning all the way unto the end.

This day–March 25–deep in the heart of Lent, we celebrate the feast of the Annunciation. The feast of God's great definitive announcement in Christ. It seems like such a strange feast to mark at this time of year when our focus is tilted toward the end of Jesus' life rather than its beginning. It almost feels artificially placed nine months before Christmas day, a far flung star from the constellation of Incarnation feasts that just happens to cross lines with the Paschal Mystery constellation. And yet, for the original Jewish Christians, such intersection was not incidental.

Ancient Jewish custom assumed that great persons were conceived and died on the same day, and there is some evidence that possibly the feast of the Annunciation preceded the feast of Christmas as an established celebration in the earliest centuries of the Church, because it was the date reckoned to be the original Good Friday. We might think this custom to be pure folklore occasioned by rare coincidence, but my suspicion is that the belief captures a deeper intuition that there is a profound connection between our birth and our death–a certain oneness and consistency to our person from beginning to end. When we celebrate the Annunciation in the midst of Lent, we recognize that the virgin birth of Christ and the death and resurrection of Christ are not two separate mysteries, but facets of the one same mystery… one same answer.

A one chord climax to the golden melody line of history:
Nothing. Nothing is impossible for your God.

Still the air vibrates with this chord as it lingers, trembling. One strong, pure harmony of pitches ringing out.

Children of Sarah, can you hear it over the din?
The orchestra is entering into its finale.
There are cymbals crashing everywhere.
Competing melodies rise and fall wailing
> God does not care.
> God is uninvolved in human history.
> God is dead.
> God does not hear your prayers.

Can you still hear God's great announcement of this day?

Listen.
In these dark days, listen carefully.

And, if it helps you in your struggle to hear,
know that this chord is accompanied by the sound of a hearty laugh.
This is not the laugh of Sarah you are hearing.
This is the last laugh.
The one that belongs to God.

11. *Aquinas Midday Prayer*
Feast of St. Angela Merici
January 27, 2004

(This was preached the day after Raymond Burke was installed as archbishop of St. Louis.)

A reading from selected passages in the counsels and last legacy of St. Angela Merici:

"I am leaving you in my place, and as my heirs, you are to have this legacy, which as my last will I give you to carry out faithfully... Strive to put into practice these few principles which I leave you to carry out after my death...."

"Be kind and compassionate.. For you will achieve more with gentleness and kindness than by harshness and cutting rebukes... Endeavor to lead by love and with a gentle and kindly hand... You must consider how greatly you must respect [those you serve]; for the more you respect them the more you will love them; the more you love them; the more care and concern you will have for them. And it will be impossible for you not to hold them... within your heart, having each one engraved there. These being done, as well as other similar things which the Holy Spirit will prompt you to do according to times and circumstances, rejoice.... And if, according to the times and circumstances, the need arises to make new rules or do something differently, do it prudently and with good advice."

"I am more alive than I ever was in this life, and I shall see you better and hold dearer the good deeds which I constantly behold you doing and I will and can help you more... The last word that I address to you, and the one I urge upon you with all the ardor of my soul, is that you live in harmony, united together in one heart and one will. Be bound to one another by bonds of charity, treating each other with respect, helping one another, bearing with one another in Christ Jesus."

"Do something
Get moving
Be confident
Risk new things

Stick with it
Get on your knees
Then be ready for 'Big surprises."

Preaching:

Yesterday, on the feast of Sts. Timothy & Titus–early bishops of the Church, friends & correspondents of the apostle Paul–we installed a new bishop in the Archdiocese of St. Louis. The celebration (having caught a piece of it on the news yesterday afternoon) appears to have been a beautiful one:

> filled with majestic music reverberating off
> the glittering mosaics of the New Cathedral;

> carefully embroidered vestments colored
> with the most treasured hues of the ecclesial rainbow;

> all the processions and pageantry that celebrate
> a flock gathered around the table with their leader,
> in unity with all of the other flocks and their leaders
> that comprise the Catholic Church.

It was a celebration in the finest fashion of the gift of order in our tradition. The hands laid upon shoulders upon shoulders upon shoulders in every generation between Timothy and Titus and Raymond that link the community of St. Louis to the community of the original Twelve. On this evening before the bright lights of the news cameras, we communicated boldly in rich symbolism to the larger public what it means for us to be Church. I am sure that we did it well.

I wish, though, that the cameras were still rolling today–on the feast of Angela Merici. Because today, in our celebration of the life and work of this treasured 15th century saint, we have yet another equally beautiful, equally important, and equally true expression of what it means to be Church. Yesterday afternoon, we celebrated the Church that is ever ancient. This morning, we celebrate the Church that is ever new.

Angela Merici was born somewhere around 1470, living her whole life in the middle of Rennaissance Italy on the eve of Trent. Although a contemporary of Michaelangelo, Luther, Copernicus, and Christopher Colombus, Angela does not seem to have been concerned or affected so much by the artistic, scientific, political, or theological intrigue of her day, as by the struggles of poor Italian families left in the wake of endless battles between various independent city-states. This was the hidden underside of Rennaissance Europe, far from the camera lights, even then.

Angela never married, instead affiliating herself with the lay Franciscans. Renowned for her charitable works and simple life style, she traveled widely on pilgrimage, seeking perhaps just the right "fit" for her life and never quite finding it. Among her trips, at least one was to Rome, where a friend arranged for her a personal audience with the pope. Asked by the pope himself if she would please settle in Rome and take leadership of an existing religious community there, she simply said, "No, that's not it; that's not quite what God's calling me to" and returned to northern Italy.

Angela was conceiving in her mind a different way of living the religious life–one that allowed women to be in direct service to the poor, living at home–not in a cloister. They would take vows; they would gather together to pray and share each other's support; they would even wear a common dress–but it would be a simple form of contemporary clothing. They would serve whatever were the most pressing needs of the community, even if it meant taking on the role of teachers–not really acceptable for women of that day; and even if it meant educating girls–who few could see the value of educating. They would not use another's rule of life; they would write their own. And, they would not be under the patronage of a men's community or even take the name of a male inspiration. They would live under the patronage of an ancient heroic woman of Christian legend–the martyr St. Ursula. Never before in the memory of the Rennaissance Church had such a thing been tried.

Angela spent the last five years of her life gathering and tending her fledgling new community, working diligently on their rule of life. Hers is the first rule that we know of written by a woman for a woman's community. And she knew that it could change and would change and should change in each and every age to meet the needs of that "time and circumstance."

In her own way, Angela represents another dimension of that "ordering" that our Church has always engaged in–reminding us that our Church is knitted together not only by the laying of hands, but also by bonds of charity, respect, and the bond that comes from simply having endured one another's quirks over a long period of time for the sake of Jesus Christ.

For every Timothy & Titus in our institution, there has also been an Angela. For every afternoon in which we celebrate God's faithful presence with us in the durable hierarchy of the Church, there is a morning after when God is just as faithfully present to us as we re-create our communities from scratch, experimenting with new ways of living the Gospel appropriate to our "time and circumstance." So says our liturgical calendar.

Not many communities could make sense of such a tradition, could live with such ambiguity and even tension. Not many communities would be able to discern that the Spirit that moved through Timothy and Titus's hands is the same Spirit that uttered "no" to the pope through Angela's lips. And to be frank, sometimes even our Church is not very good at it. But, we have something to be proud of here. For in our richly textured history, we discover that we image a God who–in the words of Augustine of Hippo–is also ever ancient and ever new.

Keep the cameras rolling.

12. Preaching for Dominican Colloquium
Dominican University, River Forest
June 2004
1 Kings 19:16, 19-21; Luke 9: 51-62

Sometimes it happens in such a subtle way that denser persons like myself might almost miss it.

I was sitting at lunch one day with Sr. Joan Delaplane–professor emeritus of Aquinas Institute. Joan, I am sure many of you know, was our preaching professor for twenty-five years, seven of which she had been my teacher and frequent lunchroom buddy. Joan decided to retire from academia in 2002. I presented my doctoral thesis in 2003.

"Have you bought robes?" she asked me over a peanut-butter sandwich.

"No," I admitted, they were a little too expensive at this point in time. I would rent them for graduation.

"I don't really need mine any more," she said. "I was wondering if you would like them."

Well now, that was mighty generous, I thought. Gratefully, I accepted and went to the office to cancel my rental order, casually explaining that I would be wearing Joan's robes instead. My colleague's eyes grew wide: *"You have inherited Joan Delaplane's mantle?"* she said.

Well, now *that* was a whole other way of looking at things, wasn't it?

Was it so?

I had been touched by *Joan's* generosity; her gracious letting go of a beloved piece of her life; a possession that she had dearly treasured for many years. It was so characteristic of the way she had acted throughout the entire transition process–clinging to nothing; embracing the future.

I had *not* reflected on what it said about *me*; on what it said about my vocation, my role, my responsibility.

I suspect that most of us have felt like Elisha at some point in time–innocently plowing our fields, all of the sudden to have the mantle of the prophet / the mantle of leadership cast over our shoulders. {For, if we had not such an event in our pasts, we probably would not be in this particular assembly today.} And, like in our first reading, we might not have been certain exactly what was happening at the time, negotiating many mixed messages:

"Did you throw your mantle over me because you see something in me you want to nurture, or just because I looked cold?"

"Did *I* throw my mantle over you?"

"Are you inviting me to apply for the job?"

"Did *I* say that I wanted you to apply?"
(Or perhaps I'm wrong and none of you have ever gotten mixed signals about your future in your institution before!)

That is the glory and the curse of symbols–we never know exactly what they mean as they so often mean so many things all at the same time.
And, it doesn't make it any easier that many of us–like Harry Potter–are only wearing invisible cloaks–mantles of responsibility; carrying the weight of a heritage, for which we have no visible symbol.

What does it mean to inherit a mantle?
How are we to live with one draped around our shoulders?
Isn't this, in some sense, what we have been pondering in our time together these past few days, as leaders of Dominican institutions?

Our experience tells us that mantles are warm and protective. They buffer us from the wicked weather of the world. A personal shelter that travels with us wherever we are.

Our experience also tells us that the warmer they are, the heavier they are. If they are not fastened well, they choke you right around the vocal chords. And give you a pain–literally–in the neck and across the shoulders.

In the Dominican tradition, the mantle was worn from September 14th– the Feast of the Triumph of the Cross–till the Gloria of the Easter

Vigil, marking a season of life set apart for penitence and interiority. Catherine of Siena belonged to a community of Dominicans so captivated by this symbol that they derived their name from it: "the Mantellate."

Scripture tells us lots of things about what it means to wear a mantle. God wears one, for starts—at one point woven of light; at another stitched of fury. On the last day, the prophet Isaiah announces, we all shall wear one—fashioned of praise, glistening with the oil of gladness.

But between the Divine Origin and the glorious end, the mantles of the Bible belong to prophets and royalty. And among these, Jesus alone wears both—

> one in his journey through the hills of Galilee; just the touch of the hem could work marvels;
> the other in the basement of Pilate's Palace to complement his crown of thorns and scepter of reed.

The mantles of scripture are things of great value and of great power—
sometimes even of the miraculous sort.
They are coveted among the booty of war.
They divide seas.
They channel fire from the heavens.
They absorb spit and mockery.
They validate authority.
They announce divine favor.

But there is one other association to note in our scriptural exploration of the symbol of the mantle; a theme front and center in our lections this morning. It is the theme of letting go, or (as I have taken to calling it) the "boiling of the sacred cows."

We see it most graphically in our reading from 1st Kings. In response to receiving Elijah's mantle, Elisha makes a bonfire of his oxen's yoke and a stew of their owners—all twelve of them. These beasts of burden were his very livelihood, his security in life, and his mark of identity as a farmer. But somehow, in coming to awareness of his call in life, he recognized them for what they were: beasts of *burden*, weights keeping him from responding freely. In letting go of them, Elisha would no longer be defined by his relationship to the land, but to the mantle. He was someone new.

We find this theme again in our Gospel reading from Luke. Jesus and his disciples have been together for a good five action-packed chapters at this point and they have come to realize with some certainty that they are Jesus' protégée–the inheritors of his mantle–and they are quite enamored with what they could do with this inheritance.

When they are refused hospitality by the Samaritans on their journey, they ask Jesus if he'd like them to call down fire and fury from the heavens, in a manner reminiscent of the action of Elijah against the false prophets of Baal and their sacrificial cows. Jesus admonishes them. They have mistaken what wearing his mantle is all about and just which cows need to be burned. He tells them that what will be smited in their new role is not their enemies but–once again–their own sense of security and identity: They will not have a place to call home. They will not have a father. They will not have a past. All the things which in the Jewish culture of the 1st century gave a person a defined sense of who they were and a structure to cling to in the chaos of the world.

I find these passages extremely challenging to me as I wrestle with what it means to live out the fullness of my vocation to prophetic leadership. I have known the warmth and the weight of the mantle. I've sensed some of its power. And, when I am open to it, I've even seen strange and wonderful things be able to happen through me, as if the strength of my predecessors was allowing me to do things I could never have done on my own. But have I entirely embraced yet all of the "letting go" inherent to this call?

In preparation for this reflection, I have taken about fourteen stabs at reconciling these passages with contemporary experience of leadership. At the end of the day, I admit with Thomas Aquinas, that I have found them all to be straw. And so, while I am tempted to share with you all the meanderings of my mind these past several weeks, I think it might be more fruitful to simply leave you with the questions that have haunted me:

What does it mean to you to count yourself among the modern-day Dominican Mantellate (in the broadest sense of the term)?

What picture from scripture or history most captivates your imagination regarding what it means to wear a mantle?

And now for the particularly hard part…

What are those messages that our *contemporary* society gives us about who we are and how we can be safe?

Which of these are compatible with a life of faithful discipleship?

Which are not?

What are the sacred cows that you have had to let go of in following your call in life?

What are the cows you still have hiding in your barn that you suspect might have to go?

How will you know?

In essence, how do you discern this?

Thomas Aquinas once said that the most fitting beatitude for students is "Blessed are they who mourn." Students laugh when they hear this; they generally think he is referring to exams and term papers. But what Thomas was referring to was the inherently paschal process of study—in which slowly all of our treasured ideas and concepts and truths are deconstructed and we feel like that which held our world together has suddenly eroded. We have the sensation of being in a free fall with nothing to cling to any more.

I suspect that Thomas would say that this is the most fitting beatitude for prophetic leaders as well. And, not because of the immense amount of paperwork and North Central accreditation. I trust you know in your gut what it is that you are invited to mourn.

And, if so, blessed are you,
Inheritors of the mantle.
Blessed are you.

13. Aquinas Midday Prayer
September 2, 2004
Luke 5:1-11

It seems like such a happy gospel:
a call along the shores of a lake
the promise of an incredible future.

Just the sort of passage that should be a joy to preach on at the beginning of a new school year, in the midst of a community that has heard *just such a call* to follow Jesus in the study of theology and the practice of ministry.

After some of the readings that the lectionary has handed me of late, I felt that I myself had landed a great catch. That is until I began to explore some of the commentaries on the call of Christ by theologians such as Dietrich Bonhoffer, who writes:
> "When Christ calls someone, he bids that person, 'Come and die.'"

Or our own beloved Thomas Aquinas who states that the most fitting beatitude for disciples of the study of theology is:
> "Blessed are they who mourn."

And it made me to ponder deeper the last words of the reading describing how the disciples parked their boats–the very same boats in which they had just experienced God's presence and abundance–and "left everything."

What is the cross of those called to theological study?
What is it that we mourn?
What is it that we park and leave?
Every vocation has a paschal journey that it must travel through which that call comes to its fullness.
What is ours?

We've been in school less than two weeks now and already a certain snicker passes through the crowd as we consider the mounds of reading piled up in the hallway just outside that door. When I took a class with Jerry Austin a couple years back, he would repeatedly remind us, and I quote, "You know that you are a graduate student when–should the recommended readings alone tumble over on you as you slept–you would be crushed, *crushed* by the weight."

Yes, there is a certain mourning here and I don't want to diminish the reality of it, but I want to speak of a more subtle and silent–even hidden–travail that sometimes characterizes the journey of those who study theology. Closer perhaps to the heart of what Thomas alludes to. And, I just want to name it aloud, because should you enter into it in the weeks to come I want you to know it, not for what it seems to be, but for what it is–a paschal journey.

It happens to everyone a little bit differently.

Sometimes it happens in studying the Bible and you begin questioning whether–if this event from Genesis didn't actually happen in history–did anything?

> Sometimes it happens in Christology, when the historical Jesus you meet looks mighty different than the one who has given you such comfort all these years.

Sometimes it happens in Church history when the papal institution we uphold we discover was also capable of something called the Cadaver Council.

> Or when the depth of the problem of theodicy really hits you for the first time.

Or when the picture of heaven you grew up with dissolves like cotton candy on a rainy day.

But, regardless of the trigger, it is a horrible moment when it feels as if everything is unraveling. One snipped thread affecting the entire web. The collapse of one conceptual domino sending all those behind it tumbling.

This is the silent travail of the theology student that Thomas speaks of: the experience of feeling like one is losing one's faith.

We came here prepared to make sacrifices for our call:

To hand over a fair chunk of change.
To live on a diet of Ramen noodles and peanut butter sandwiches.
To endure the confusion and perhaps ribbing of some of our friends and family members.
And, in some cases, willing even to handover our lives to God in whatever way might be demanded of us.

Never in our worst nightmares did we expect that we might have to let go of our conceptions of the God who drew us here in the first place; abandoning the boats, the vehicles in which we first heard our calls.

Blessed are they who mourn.

+++++++

"The intellectual discipline of our study has this ultimate purpose," writes Timothy Radcliffe, former master of the Order of Preachers, "to bring us to this moment of conversion when our false images of God are destroyed so that we may draw near to the mystery."

There will be times that we will be tempted to recoil from that mystery because it is so much larger, deeper, and murkier than we were able to see from the boat. And we will want to return to our previous life in which our world made sense and we knew who God was. And some of us might and that is okay because it means that God has a different paschal journey for us, a different way to draw us near.

But if you find somewhere within yourself the strength to remain in the murky, opaque waters of unknowing
> and yet still get to your knees each morning,
> and yet still sit humbly before this deconstructed but holy word,
> and yet still gather around this scandalized but sacred table
> and hope—this is key: and *hope*

Then know that God has placed within you the heart of a theologian.
And that you are not losing your faith at all.
You are finding it.
This is the paschal journey of your very particular vocation.
And "Do not be afraid," Jesus whispers to those willing to follow.
"Do not be afraid."

14. *Aquinas Midday Prayer*
All Souls' Day
November 2, 2004
2nd Maccabees & John 6:37-40

When I was a junior in college, as some of you already know, I spent six months abroad as an exchange student in Sierra Leone, a tiny country in West Africa. There were nine of us who participated in the program–all between the ages of 19 and 21. Each of us went for a variety of reasons:

> to experience what it is like to be a minority (or in one case–a majority);
> to learn about other cultures;
> to see new things;

And, (if we were entirely honest) to have the opportunity to recreate ourselves from scratch. I am not sure we *would* be entirely honest, if confronted with this motive point blank, but it was there–most certainly so in myself.

All of us wish to be someone a little bit different than we already are–a little more carefree; a little less neurotic; a little more daring; a little less shy. All of us have relationships we would rather escape than understand; issues we would rather avoid than address.

There is a something about making a radical break that really appeals to us. We can start again anew. "Go West, young man." Move to another country. Enter a religious order. Change careers. Run for office.

The problem is that when we attempt such a re-creation, we often discover in a most painful manner the truth of the old axiom, "Wherever you go, you take yourself with you."

Here the nine of us were in our first weeks of life in a foreign land and we were not new people, we were more ourselves than we had ever been before. More neurotic, less daring, more shy. Relationships could be severed by distance, but their effects were still there. And the patterns of relating were still the same. Issues that seemed like minor personality quirks back in the U.S. suddenly blossomed as if force fed Miracle Gro.

Really, the axiom should read, "Wherever you go, you take *twice* yourself with you." And, for some of us, that is very heavy luggage indeed.

Today, we commemorate the feast of All Souls. The last in a triduum of days that kicks off a new season of sorts in the liturgical year. Like its mirror in the peak of Spring, this little triduum at the peak of Fall includes a day in which we dwell in the dark world of death, a day in which we celebrate the resurrection of the body of Christ, and an in-between kind of day when what is going on inside that tomb is somewhat of a mystery.

The difference between these two tridua is that the order of the days is somewhat mixed. In the autumn, the "in-between sort of day" does not come in-between at all, but last.

The triduum of Jesus Christ has a beginning, a middle, and an end.

The triduum of his Risen Body has a beginning, an end, and a middle.

It has all the same refrains, all the same chords, all the same words. *It is* the same mystery both celebrate. But, at the end of this triduum we are left hanging on a different note to reflect upon. A haunting little hum with lyrics that go something like this: "Wherever you go, you take yourself with you."

For, the experience of death, in the Catholic tradition, is a little like crossing the border of a foreign land. The good news of our faith is that death is not the end that it seems that it is. The web of relationships that ties us to our kin and neighbors is not erased. Our personal uniqueness is not obliterated. Even in this journey into the most opaque mystery encountered by humankind, we take ourselves with us.

On the other hand, the bad news of our faith–if that is permissible to say–is that death isn't the end that it seems to be. The web of relationships that ties us to our kin and neighbors is not erased. Our personal uniqueness is not obliterated. We take ourselves with us, perhaps doubly so. For on the other side, we are without the masks, without the coping mechanisms, without the distractions we can hide behind here.

In death, we are more fully ourselves
than we ever knew ourselves to be.
That is good.
And, that is bad.
For, we are very complex beings.

This Catholic intuition about an in-between state bridging this life and the next is very old. We know that in the 2nd century accounts of Sts. Perpetua and Felicity, early Christians were already conceiving of a state of purgation for those whose hearts were not quite so single as those of the martyrs. And, in fact, some find a sense of such a state even earlier–in the Old Testament book of 2nd Maccabees that is offered in the lectionary as a possible reading for today's feast.

The concept of purgatory has taken some hard knocks over the centuries because of abuses with indulgences and whatnot. It has always seemed strange in our larger American culture, which tends to view death in very individualistic and final terms. In recent years, even Catholics have struggled with this long-lived belief. Do we still believe in purgatory and limbo? Doesn't St. Paul refer to all the baptized as saints? Why do we pray for the dead–aren't they already in heaven or (god forbid) hell? Haven't they suffered enough in this world? Why would a good and forgiving God have them suffer in the next?

And yet, the longer I sit with this doctrine and this day, the more I am moved by how very relevant and revealing our intuition about this "in-between state" is.

It speaks to me of a God who is so patient and merciful that He's willing to keep working with us on the other side of death. Who respects human persons so deeply that He does not fix them in a flash like some sort of machine, but works with them in their own healing, in their own time, helping them open themselves to more and more love.

It speaks to me of a beautiful vision of the human person that is not individualistic (concerned with the forgiveness of my personal sins for the sake of my personal salvation) but rather communal (concerned with healing all the ways in which sin has impacted our relationships for the sake of the salvation of the whole Body of Christ).

It speaks to me of a profound interrelatedness of all the baptized–that none of us will fully rest in peace until we all do.

It speaks to me of a Church that is okay living with the mysteriousness of the Paschal journey; okay with not entirely knowing what exactly is going on inside that tomb, but confident about where it is heading.

This day of remembrance can be very consoling to us, especially as we recall the many loved ones that we have watched crossed over the border of death in the past year. It is comforting to be able to place them in the gentle, transforming hands of God. To know that we can still pray for them. That our relationships with them can still be healed.

And yet, at the same time, this day of remembrance can be very challenging. For, if our Catholic intuition about purgatory is true, it has implications for the living as well as the dead. It means that while death is not the terror we might perceive it to be; neither is it the panacea. Our divisions and wounds will not be erased by a magical divine wand, but by a God who accompanies us in the difficult, sometimes painful process of reconciliation, forgiveness, and healing. We can engage reconciliation in this life and/or in the next, but either way we are going to have to engage it—because this is the way that we know God to work. In the face of a culture that says, "Live it up! You can't take it with you!", the Church says, "Work it out, because you will!"

Today, as we pray for all the faithful departed passing through the mystery of the "in-between," let us also pray for ourselves who are living that same mystery of reconciliation and healing in our own lives and world.

For we need not wait till death to work things out. We need not wait to death to experience God's mercy, to enter into deeper communion with God.

We can enter into a state of purgation now.

We can open our hardened and hurting hearts
to the tenderness of God now.
We do not need to go anywhere else to know such care.
Wherever we go, God is there.

15. Aquinas Midday Prayer
January 18, 2005
Mark 2: 23-28

In the atrium, there is a presentation that we do with children around the age of nine that is called "The Cosmic Maxims." The presentation invites the nine year olds to look at the world around them. No, really look....

At the sun. Does it decide when to rise and when to set? Or is its appearance so predictable that we can print in the newspaper each morning the very minute we can expect light on the horizon?

And the moon. Is it there one night and not the next? Or is there a pattern to its waxing and waning? A thin scythe in the sky at one point in the month, we can count the days with certainty till it becomes a full circle of light.

And the tides. And the constellations. And the seasons.

There is a set of unwritten laws that guide everything in creation from the movement of the stars to the tiniest flower of the fields which blossoms at one certain time of the year and no other.

Without these laws, nothing could exist. With them, all things work together in an amazing harmony that makes life on this planet not only possible, but prosperous, abundant, extravagant. All of nature obeys these laws without resistance—laws so intricate and complex that humanity has not yet discovered their every nuance, much less been able to replicate them. It seems these unwritten laws emanate forth from an intelligence much greater than our own, an intelligence motivated only by love for this world, only by the desire to see it flourish.

Is it only the plant and animal kingdoms though that have been given a set of laws to follow? Only the planets and stars? Are we, too, to enjoy this harmony? Do we have a role in the flourishing of all life? Are there laws to which we, too, must acquiesce? If so, what are they?

Aaah–that is the million dollar question, isn't it? Pause on the presentation to the nine year olds and let us rest here for a moment, because it is a relevant and contested question indeed. While a small percentage of the population that counts itself as hedonists or anarchists might deny any such predetermined laws for humans, the great percentage of all cultures across all times have devoted themselves intentionally to discover what these laws might be.

Politicians considering stem cell research.
Environmentalist looking at population growth.
Judges wanting to post the decalogue in the court.
Philosophers & Physicists.
Native healers and doctors.
Astronomers and ethicists.

All seeking to discern, to the best of their ability, the laws that would give clarity to our role in the order of things. Perhaps better than any other image, this perennial yearning for guidance and direction is captured in the quest of the young scholar of law who kneels at the feet of Jesus and queries,

> "Teacher, *what must I do* to enjoy eternal life, to enjoy the *full flourishing* of life?"

Jesus tells him to hunt within the wisdom of his people, a people long dedicated to understanding God's law. What does it say? What is at the core?

And the young lawyer replies, "Love the Lord your God with all your heart, with all your soul, with all your strength, and with all your mind. Love your neighbor as you love yourself."

"That is correct," Jesus glows. Love. "Do this and you shall live."

Humans are the quirkiest of creatures in the universe, for the only law by which they are called to live is at one time both the simplest and the most complex. Love. Made in the image of God, the "Intelligence of Love," the only thing they are asked to do is to live in the image of God, with every one of their acts motivated only by love.

We have so much freedom, it is downright frightening.

Would that you could print in the newspaper the rising and setting of love, the schedule by which it is to wax and wane each month.

Would that you could say, "At this minute, love will always do this. At that moment, love will always do that."

No, we can describe what love generally will look like; we can note that over time we have discovered this kind of response to a situation to be the most loving response, but these are only really good guidelines.

The only law in the end is love and it has a hundred different faces, most often with expressions of kind tenderness or concern, but also occasionally fierce or angry.

I say all this as a very long prelude to a very short reflection on a very sticky gospel–today's gospel reading from Mark. In this passage, the Pharisees could come off as excessively nosy neighbors, so concerned about Jesus following every dot and tittle of Jewish law that they apparently break the Sabbath themselves to spy on what he and his disciples are doing in the field. And, Jesus could come off as one of those rare hedonists or anarchists who views all law as disposable, or at least adaptable to suit one's own purposes.

In contrast, I think the Pharisees, much like ourselves, possess a deep desire to live in harmony with God's will. They want the fullness of life and they recognize that this is only possible through obedience to God's law for us. But, also like ourselves, they would like more clarity, more sureness that they are doing what is right, than perhaps the law of love allows.

They would like to be the sun, with directions about what time to rise. What time to set. An exact percentage of income that must be given to charity. A point in the Mass by which one must arrive in order to fulfill the Sunday obligation. The Pharisees, much like ourselves perhaps, would like to be able to codify love. To have a pre-nuptial agreement with life. "I would like to know exactly what is going to be asked of me in this relationship."

Jesus, though, the Gospels consistently tell us, just does not think in these terms. Neither a hedonist nor an anarchist, he, too, possesses a deep desire to live in harmony with God's will. He, too, wants to be entirely obedient to God's law. But, unlike the Pharisees, he does not covet the certainty of the moon or the stars with their fixed cycle of behaviors. He embraces fully the role of the human in the universe, to live fully in the image of God, to have every action motivated only by love. So much freedom, it was frightening.

Because lots of Saturdays, love told him to observe the Sabbath.
But sometimes on Saturday, it told him to heal a man with a withered arm or pluck grain from a field.

And lots of Tuesdays, love told him to announce the forgiveness of sin, but it also made him purge the temple market.

And lots of Fridays, love told him to preach the good news of the Kingdom, but one Friday it told him to die.

And lots of Sundays, love told him to sleep in late with his buddies.
But one Sunday it told him to rise.

Jesus knew only one law in life.
It was the law to which all true law is ordered.
He wishes the same for us.

16. Aquinas Midday Prayer
September 7, 2005
Luke 6:20-26

(Preached the week after Hurricane Katrina in New Orleans.)

Café Du Monde sits right up next to the Mississippi River. As mighty barges and waterfowl pass by, you can drink world-renowned coffee, surpassed in fame only by the café's fried beignets. You can buy a box of powdered mix from the market nearby, as you shop for fiery hot Tabasco, dirty rice, and alligator pie, but beignets never taste as good when you make them at home as when you eat them in the French Quarter.

I have been to New Orleans a number of times over the last several years—twice for conferences, once to persuade a field education intern why late-night "ministry" on Bourbon Street wasn't a very prudent idea, and a couple times to visit my sister who lived a short trolley ride down St. Charles Ave. One of the last times I was there, we came across a pre-Mardi Gras day parade with the most vulgar float I have ever seen in my entire life. Crew members dressed up as nuns and priests were inevitably involved, several of whom walked up and "snogged" my sister while showering her with beads. Not one approached me. I couldn't figure out whether to be grateful or offended.

It is hard to imagine that this scene is all underwater, looted, or thick with sewage now, like a snapshot out of Noah's world. My sister arrived on a flight from Houston late last Thursday night with about 6 pairs of clothes and all her photographs, but not much else. And, of course, she is one of the luckiest ones.

I suspect there are a few right now who could read today's Gospel and note that the City of Sin and Obscene Floats has simply gotten its due like Sodom & Gomorrah of old. Not long ago, I met some preachers of this persuasion in New Orleans itself—calling mostly curious tourists to repentance. "Woe to those who laugh now, for you shall grieve and weep." Well, I suppose you could look at it that way.

But most, I would guess, hear today's Gospel and focus not on the second half, but the first, wondering what exactly it means that the poor are "blessed" when they are sleeping upright in a stadium chairs for the 5th night in a row in a sweltering Superdome;

what exactly it means that the mourning are "blessed" when they still can't figure out where their loved ones could be;

what exactly it means that the hungry are "blessed" when not only food but clean water has run out.

In the Greek, the word for "blessed" is "makarios." Originally, it referred to the happy state of the gods and the dead who were above earthly sufferings and labors. Later it came to refer to the wealthy, who like the divine and the deceased, did not have to worry about the things others did. In the Old Testament, there are a variety of "macarisms" or "beatitudes", especially in the Wisdom literature. Persons were considered "blessed" if they had a wife, children, beauty, health, riches, honor, and/or wisdom. Jesus' beatitudes, however, turn this pattern on its head. Jesus is naming as blessed those who society never considered blessed: the poor, the hungry, the persecuted, the grieving.

For Jesus, these persons were "makarios" not because they led lives of leisure, but because they were assured a share in the Kingdom of God which Jesus likely anticipated arriving very soon. Scripture scholars have spilt much ink on the question, "Why them?" Perhaps it was because the poor and grieving lived more authentically the role of the human in the world, recognizing that we really have very little control over things and are all ultimately dependent on the goodness of God. Perhaps it was because, like Jesus, the persecuted and starving so hungered for the coming of God's Kingdom. The wealthy and prominent, who were served well by the status quo, had no real desire for the social order to change. For them it came at great cost, but for the outcasts, there was nothing to lose.

Or perhaps these persons were "makarios" simply because they had a special place in God's heart. Like the parent with several healthy, gifted children and one disabled or struggling little one, the little one receives extra attention and care. Not because the parent doesn't love all the children, but because for all to flourish *equally*, this one will need *unequal tenderness*. This one tugs in a particular way on the parent's heart.

In a time when the promise of the Kingdom does not appear to be quite as imminent as in Jesus' day, the assurance that the hurting of the earth are the object of special divine care can feel a little anemic. When I asked my sister whether the beatitudes were any consolation to her at this time, she replied, "If they are saying that my neighbors and I have to wait till heaven to see any of these come true, then no, that doesn't really make me feel any better at all." She spoke like the man screaming into the television camera, "We are tired of hearing that help is on the way. Where is it *now?*"

Was there any way in the present that she did feel blessed?, I persisted. Long pause. Well, there was a man in a coffee shop in Houston who, when he found out that she was from New Orleans, did not charge her for the coffee. She paused again. And, there was an old teacher from high school who sent a card for her to my parent's house with a $100 bill inside. Another pause and then a litany began to tumble forth: There were our parents who gave her their credit card to book a flight and our four-year-old nephew who drew her a picture of the rain going away and her house having sun over it again. And me, who treated her to dinner and wine while pestering her with what she considered silly questions about the Beatitudes that only religious people would think about at a time like this. Having given up on religion herself many years back, she nevertheless described an "unequal tenderness" of the divine sort that had been mediated to her by family, friends, and even strangers throughout her painful sojourn.

A Kingdom incomplete, for certain, but in progress.

A God with stumbling human hands and feet.

A mystery so deep, we suffer from bends before we reach the bottom.

An answer not entirely satisfying, but perhaps all that we and the blessed of the Kingdom have to cling to in the present time.

17. *Aquinas Midday Prayer*
March 7, 2006
Matt. 6: 7-15

For our bedtime reading of late, my son Micah and I have been exploring a book on the history of the universe. It all began about the size of a mustard seed, if scientists are correct, approximately 13.7 billion years ago.

In the opening second of time, this universe seed was 10 to the 72nd power denser than water. That is 10–comma–with 71 zeroes after it.

Within a fraction of its first second, it exploded to "10–comma–51 zeroes-after-it"- times its original size, the size of a galaxy. From mustard seed to galaxy in the time that it takes to say "1 Mississi…"

Within this same first second, the energy was converted into particles and anti-particles, almost equal in number, instantaneously canceling each other out. But, for every 1 million anti-particles, there were 1 million and one particles. And it is this small remnant of particles, only 1-200 millionth of the matter from the original blast, that makes up all of the galaxies that exist today.

Not immediately, of course; it took about 1 billion years till the first galaxy formed. Our own Milky Way galaxy didn't come together until the year "2 billion." We cannot be sure how many stars comprise it. Best guess is about 100 billion, only 5000 or so of which we can see with the naked eye. What we can see of our galaxy is equivalent in proportion to a handful of sand in comparison to a beach. Our own star, the sun, did not emerge until about 8 billion years after the Big Bang. And, our earth another 500 million years after that.

At this point in the reading, I grew quiet. My mind was still stuck on figuring out how many zeroes came after the decimal point in 1-200 millionth. I was lost in a sea of awe before something I couldn't quite wrap my mind around. Breaking the silence, Micah said, "But I need to know, what was before that seed?"

We all do, don't we?

++++++++++++

"The Kingdom of God is like a mustard seed which someone took and sowed in a field..."

How do you name a Someone who sows stars like grain? How to you relate to Someone with an embrace 156 billion light years wide?

Today, Jesus teaches us how to name, how to relate. He teaches us how to pray.

Jesus begins by contrasting his prayer with that of the "pagans"–those unfamiliar with the God of Abraham. When they stood and looked up at the midnight sky, they perceived a Someone far, far away who reigned over a stable and changeless universe, following a staid, circular pattern of seasons over and over and over again. They needed to speak their every need because otherwise, this distant Someone wouldn't know what those needs were. This made their prayers very long.

Jesus, in contrast, names this Someone "Father"–making the remarkable claim that the one who knows the name of each and every of the 100 billion Milky Way stars, also knows the name of each and every of the 6.5 billion human beings that inhabit one mere planet in this galaxy, and the number of hairs each has on its head. Tenderly involved in each of our lives, we don't need to utter many words because this Someone already knows every one of our needs–all of which can, hence, be succinctly summed up in a petition for "our daily bread."

The heart of Jesus' prayer, then, will not be about making the Father aware of our situation, but making us aware of the Father's situation. Making us aware of the Father's dreams for his mustard seed kingdom. A kingdom that Jesus, when looking up at the heavens, perceived as neither staid nor circular but stirring and spiraling. A universe still in the process of being created, not yet finished, moving toward a fullness that he had not yet seen but had trained himself to long for with every ounce of his being.

As humans, in Jesus' worldview, we are not passive consumers of whatever the universe dishes out; we are actors, invited to be collaborators in seeing God's Kingdom toward its completion.

The purpose of prayer, Jesus taught, is not to open up God to our dreams, but to open up ourselves to God's dreams. *Thy Kingdom come; thy will be done.*

Do we have any idea what we are asking for here?
Jesus and the prophets give us lots of clues as to what this will look like for our planet:

The sick will be healed, the blind will see, the lame will walk, yes,
Lions will lay down with lambs.
But also
The last will be first.
Those who only worked the last shift will get a full day's wage.
We will be table mates with tax collectors and
prostitutes and heretics from Samaria.
Mountains will be leveled and valley raised.
Crosses will need to be taken up
And we will die before we will rise.
Is this really what we want to see happen?
Are we willing to be agents of its coming?

Do we have *any* idea what we are asking for?

When we stand before a God for whom a billion years is like a day and say, "Here, use me"?

When we call out to a Father who can turn a mustard seed into a universe in single second....

Why not ask lightening to strike us directly?

It is a dangerous way to pray indeed. The next time we will hear Jesus uttering this phrase, he is sweating blood in the Garden of Olives struggling to remain open to the Kingdom: *"Not my will, but thine be done."*

Is it any wonder that the rubrics of the old Latin Mass asked if we "dare" to pray it?

And yet, in the ancient tradition of the Church, we are invited to pray it with arms outstretched, in the *orans* position. A position that conveys openness, a lack of both possessiveness or protectiveness, a posture of vulnerability.   A posture not unlike that of Jesus on the cross. *"Thy Kingdom come; thy will be done."*

This is how Jesus says we are to name the Someone who existed before the beginning of time.
This is how he invites us to be in relationship.
This is how he tells us to pray.
Do *you* dare?

18. *Aquinas Midday Prayer*
May 2, 2006
John 6:30-35

When I was a child, I remember being very perplexed by the stories of the risen Jesus and why no one could recognize him. Mary Magdalene. Cleopas and his companion on the road to Emmaus. Peter and friends fishing along the coast. Clearly there was some kind of problem here. When I was about nine, I remember my mom responding that probably they couldn't recognize him because they were crying and their vision was blurred. "All of them?" I thought. When I was about eleven, my parish priest told me that Jesus was probably wearing different clothes. That seemed particularly lame.

A few years ago, when I asked Don Goergen, in specific reference to the Mary Magdalene account, he said that it was because Jesus came back in the form of a rabbit. When Mary Magdalene recognized who it was, she called out "Rabbit!" but a later textual gloss by an errant monk had changed it to read "Rabboni!" Obviously, I shouldn't be looking for answers from a man who thinks his bunny is cuter and smarter than my son.

And yet every year in the first week of Easter, all of these stories fill the lectionary again, begging the question. One after another, day after day, letting us know that when Jesus rose from the dead, none of those closest to him could recognize him. Why was that?

It strikes me, after these many years of pondering, that perhaps the simplest answer is that he didn't look anything like he did before he died. Obviously, he looked like an ordinary human: Mary Magdalene thought he was a gardener. Cleopas thought he was a fellow traveler. I have to think they'd have noticed if he was glowing or shimmering or something. But he didn't have the same physical features as he had before. The way they recognized the mystery person was Jesus was that he did something that they had known to be characteristic of him. For Mary, when she heard her name spoken, it became clear to her who this was. For Thomas, it was in the act of touching wounds. For Cleopas, it was the breaking of bread. For Peter, it was the abundance of a catch.

Here begins the disciples' boot camp for living in a post-resurrection world. Jesus needs to initiate his friends into a new way of being in relationship with him that isn't based on the sense of sight. He needs to train them to recognize that it's him present even when they can't tell it's him with their eyes. Like pilots being trained for low-flying night missions, they need to learn to listen for faint beeps and echoes, to read the signs, to trust the instruments, to hone their intuition. To fly by faith.

Every year, the readings of this season put disciples of today through this same boot camp. After being clued into Jesus' new approach to "being present" during the first week of the season, we, too, are asked to (metaphorically) "close" our eyes and begin to train to recognize him as with us still even when we cannot see him. During last week, we heard Jesus speaking of his presence in a baptism of water and spirit. We heard him speak about being light in the darkness. We heard of him present when testimony is given on his behalf. Now this week, we hear him spoken of, for several days in a row, as living bread.

The people in today's Gospel ask, "What sign can you do, that we may *see* and believe in you?" But everything about this season, ironically, is about being given signs so that we can *not* see and still believe. Everything about this season is about learning to fly by faith.

Sometimes theologians talk about this kind of vision–or perhaps I should say 'non-vision'- as "sacramental imagination." The ability to know the Risen Christ near when the Word is spoken, when our name is called, when we touch a wound, when we taste him as living bread, when we go deep into the waters of baptism. This kind of imagination is central to the Catholic worldview. For if we do not stretch our capacities to perceive him in wine and bread, what practice shall we have to recognize him present in the homeless man searching through the dumpster for aluminum cans, the neighbor who always takes our parking space, or the classmate/colleague who "gets our goat."

If it were easy to develop a sacramental imagination, we'd have seen the fullness of God's reign a long time ago. I doubt we would wage war on people who we were able to perceive as the living body of Christ. We would not have been able to have a holocaust in Germany. We would not be able to have genocide in Rwanda or Darfur. We would not be able to abort a child, to put to death a criminal, to segregate a school or an economy based on race.

But sacramental imagination is not something easy to come by. Not for the first disciples wandering the burial grounds outside Jerusalem or sailing on the waves of the Sea of Tiberias. And not for us today. And so every year, again, we enter into this boot camp. We sit with these readings of the Easter season. And we ask once again, to learn to recognize Jesus' presence in new ways; learn what it means to fly by faith.

19. Aquinas Midday Prayer
November 7, 2007
Luke 14:25-33

The college at which I did my undergrad degree was fairly well known in the sciences. Lots of people when they went there listed "Pre-Med" as their intended major. We had a couple of immensely popular biology teachers on the faculty and they were known to do fun, creative things to help make their classes enjoyable and thought-provoking. For example, one was known to drink eggs raw and eat insects in front of his class... you know that sort of thing. Their classes were burgeoning–especially freshman year. Even non-science majors would take them just for the experience. Some of these freshman classes were lighter weight, like one course nicknamed "Rocks for Jocks."

But then, sophomore year, there was "Zoology." It was known within the department as the "weeder-outer" course. The crowds of potential doctors had been building up for two semesters now and it was time to separate the chaff from the grain, as they say. Unfortunately, I was one of those history majors who didn't get the message in time. I was there to watch teachers swallow raw eggs.

Let's just say that after week after week of phyla and genus and dissection of every type of carcass, the class of 100 was down to about 60 and I consider myself very lucky to have pulled off a low B.

Today's reading strikes me as the Gospel parallel to Zoology 101. We are fourteen chapters into the book of Luke and during this period of time, the crowds have been building. "Great crowds" it says were following Jesus. He's preaching brilliantly. Worked a few miracles. I don't know–maybe swallowed a raw egg or two–and the people are digging it. This is the one to be with. The guru to follow.

And then, it says, Jesus turns around. I love the phraseology here: he turns around. He looks out over this massive pool of candidates for the position of disciple that has been assembling. "This has gotten a little out of control," you can hear him thinking. It is time to do some winnowing. So right then and there, he offers his "Weeding Out" lecture.

"This is all fine and good," he says. "I am really glad that you are all here. But I have to tell you something. If you want to be my disciple, there are these three things that I feel compelled to let you know about:

"One, you have to hate your family. Mother, father, sister, brother, kids, spouse. All of them. Yes, I know that your family is the main way that you identify yourself here. It's how you know who you are. But, that can't be any more. You've got to identify with me.

"Two, you've got to take up your cross. You've got to be willing to deny yourself, even let go of your own life. It's true, you could die. I want you to know that.

"Oh, and then, #3, you need to let go of all your possessions. Just get rid of them.

"And, I want you to think hard about these things because you don't want to get half way into this discipleship thing and then change your mind. Just like the builder of a home or the leader of an army. You don't dig the basement and then not have enough money to complete the house. It'd be useless. Or you don't go off and invade a country and then find out you don't have the soldiers or supplies you needed and have to beg for peace. No, if you're going to be my disciple, make sure you're in for the long haul. That's it. Class dismissed. On Monday, we'll be talking about salt that has lost its flavor."

And you can kind of seeing them walking home with their notebooks, can't you? That sort of deer-in-the-headlights look. Maybe a few grumblers, mumbling, "Well that's not really fair." "Was that in the syllabus?" "Do you think I can drop this course and still get my money back or will there be a permanent incomplete on my transcript?"

And come Monday morning, who dares to show back up? My guess is four groups of students. In the first row is the poor, who have never had any possessions of which to let go and are glad not to have been disqualified on this account. The second row is filled with those who have never had much of a family in the first place—at least not one that loved as it ought—and would really like to form a new sort of community. The third row is comprised of the long suffering, who've known the cross and do not fear it any longer. They know there is nothing more that the world has to offer them.

And then bringing up the rear are the theologians. Jesus raises his eyebrows when they return. He knows that they are prone to rationalizing his words. And they know that Jesus is prone to use hyperbole in his. Isn't this the man who elsewhere told us to pluck out our eyes and cut off our hands if they were the source of sin? They are back and they have some questions:

> Um, what exactly do you mean by "hate"?
>
> If you hate someone, don't they become your enemy?
>
> And, didn't you say to love your enemies?
>
> If everyone were to give up all of their possessions, who would be responsible for carrying for property? Isn't it true that communities thrive better when there is private ownership than not?
>
> What would happen to children if abandoned by their parents? Wouldn't that only create more poverty and suffering rather than less?

Jesus knows that really they should be history majors. These are the students whose only hope of salvation comes through their persistence. If they continue to show up maybe–by the grace of God–they can pull a low B. They are never going to be the top students in the class, but at least they are there.

And Jesus looks over this class with love. Now it is beginning to look less like a crowd and more like a church. The poor, the suffering, the truly "home-less," the questioner. These are the people for whom he came. This is a group he can work with.

20. *Aquinas Midday Prayer*
January 10, 2008
Luke 4:14-22

Wow. So here we are again at the start of a new semester, ready to try once again to live out the crazy mission of Aquinas Institute of Theology to be a graduate school of theology *and* ministry. It doesn't sound so crazy to those of you who are joining the community for the first time, does it? But wait till you try it.

Most schools tend lean in one direction or another–they define themselves primarily as a school of theology *or* a school of ministry. The schools of theology see their work as the pursuit of truth, wherever that might take them. It is an academic and heady endeavor and, to be quite honest, that pastoral stuff is a little fluffy, lightweight. The schools of ministry see themselves as readying people to serve the Church, to be attentive to the needs of the People of God and, quite frankly, that theology stuff is a tad esoteric, not very practical or relevant to real life.

And then there is Aquinas Institute–crazy enough to think that both theology and ministry are absolutely critical. Can't pick one or the other. Crazy enough to claim that theology and ministry fit together hand in glove. Crazy enough to claim that its graduates are to be pastorally-grounded theologians…. And theologically-grounded pastors.

What do we even call these people? Ministogians? Theolinisters? What will these creatures look like? How can we hold it all together?

Today's Gospel from Luke gives us an image of what the "Ministogian" looks like. An image that we can cling to as we try to live our mission as a school this new semester. It is the image of Jesus, in the synagogue at Nazareth. Jesus who, like us, is on the brink of a new adventure in his life. Jesus illuminating what it means to "put it all together."

The first thing that Jesus does in the synagogue, according to Luke, is receive the scroll of Isaiah the prophet. He takes into his hands the tradition of his people, accepts what is being passed on to him. This is the first movement of any "ministogian"–to learn, to receive, to accept.

Theology is all about the passing on of a tradition–something that is not only a noun but a verb, not only words, but the act of speaking. One hand touching another with the Word of God passing between them. Receiving a tradition requires openness, humility, curiosity, a willingness to learn, a willingness to be in relationship with the one passing tradition on.

I wonder how Jesus received the words of the prophet. I imagine two hands outstretched. These scrolls were quite weighty things, in every sense of the word. I wonder if he held them at a bit of a distance, with reverence, before him, or if scooped them into his arms and pressed them against his heart. I don't know. Makes us wonder how we will receive.

But, we do know this: when he came to the stand and rested the scroll upon it, it says that he searched through it.

In Jesus' time, scholars think that synagogue services always included a reading from the Torah and from the prophets, but there wasn't a lectionary per se. Jesus had to look within the words of the prophet to choose the particular passage that he wanted to lift up that day. And, I wonder if this isn't always the second task of the "ministogian"–to discern. To take the tradition and search within it. For while all of it belongs to us and none of it should be lost, there is an act of judgment involved:

What is most valuable for today?
What is most essential to remember in this time?
What is most meaningful in this age?

This work of discernment is possibly the trickiest task of the theologian. It requires a deep knowledge of the tradition and also a deep knowledge of the people in front of you, of the time in which you live.

For his congregation on that day, Jesus chose the beginning of Isaiah, chapter 61. This was probably at the end of the scroll so he may have searched for quite some time to find just the right words. I wonder where our search is going to lead us to and how we will know when we've found what we are looking for, and on what grounds. Some of us could think "this" is the most important thing to proclaim; some of us could think "that" is more needed in our time. You can see why this is the trickiest task of the ministogian, and why in a community of ministogians this task requires the most dialogue.

But "this" or "that," we remember that Jesus didn't keep what he'd searched for to himself. He proclaimed it. And, here we have the third task of the ministogian. Sharing God's word with others. It is interesting because this is the only evidence that we have in the Gospels that Jesus was able to read. His ability to do this gives witness to long hidden years of study that preceded his preaching. The work of theology flowers in the proclamation of the Word.

What do you imagine his voice sounded like as he read? Was it booming? Or did he read in whispering awe of the words he'd discovered in the scroll? Maybe he spoke with piercing intensity... or maybe he was laughing because it was such good news he had to share. We can wonder... about his voice, and about what ours will sound like.

And, then, Jesus sits and for the first time in the whole narrative, he speaks in his own words. Many times, it would seem that the less we know about something, the more we say about it. And the more we know about something, the fewer words we'll need to get our point across.

Jesus gives perhaps one of the shortest homilies ever given in human history: "Today, this scripture passage is fulfilled in your hearing."

Jesus knows—and (we can guess) knows deeply—that through him, God's promises of long ago will be actualized. They will come into reality. The poor will hear good news. The captives and oppressed will be set free. The blind will see. A year of jubilee will be celebrated.

We find here the last great task of the ministogian—serving the actualization of God's reign in our time. Making God's promises real through the work of our hands, our feet, our hearts. It is not enough to proclaim the Word; we must do the Word.

The model that Jesus gives us in this passage—receiving, discerning, proclaiming, actualizing—is a powerful one. It gives us a clue about how we, too, as a community, can hold together these critical aspects of our common call to be both pastoral theologians and theological pastors. Some of us will excel or focus on one of these tasks more than the other, but all of us are called to embrace in some way all four.

Luke says that the people who encountered Jesus that day found his words to be graceful. We could read this in a couple different ways. Yes, definitely, these words were pleasing, they were eloquent. But we could also say that they mediated for the people an experience of grace. An experience of God among them.

May our life together this semester be grace for the world.

21. Aquinas Midday Prayer
January 23, 2008
1 Samuel 17:32-33, 37, 40-51

Here is a story that has been one of my favorites since my first summer at the free Lutheran vacation bible school that my mom sent us to when we were kids. Of course, the story (as told there in cute cartoon cut-outs) had largely been excised of the gore and violence. None of the trash talking about "dogs" and "leaving your corpse out for the birds" that makes David and Goliath sound like they belong in the NBA. Just the core story line about the small defeating the powerful and mighty, the little one conquering the great with God at their side.

I suspect that it is a favorite of "little people" everywhere, and by this term, I do not just mean children. We all can see ourselves in the place of David. Confronted with a giant evil that seems so *big*, so much bigger than ourselves. We know what it feels like to be alone, raging against forces more powerful than we are. And, there is something so consoling about this story. So hopeful. Because we hear that God stands behind the underdog, and with God all things are possible. One well aimed shot from the sling of a shepherd boy can end the oppression of a nation.

I remember a few years ago in working on the publication of a book, I became embroiled in a battle with a theologian appointed by the cardinal of an unnamed archdiocese over a matter of canon law. Here I was armed with my one little semester of canon law class against a big publishing company that–at least from where I sat–appeared invincible.... And I won. I remember in midday prayer right around that time, hearing this very reading from the lectionary, and thinking "Hah! It's true! Goliath bites the dust!"

I hope that you've known that kind of vindication in some of your darker hours when you have felt very small.

At the same time, in more recent years, I've become aware–shockingly– that not everyone thinks of me as a ruddy, youthful David with God on my side. Somehow, without my being terribly conscious of it happening, the little girl in vacation bible school grew quite big.

Became a teacher.
Became an administrator.
Became a mom ... of a tween-ager.
Became a voting citizen of the most powerful nation on earth.

And even though I still often think of myself as being the tiny underdog against the evils of life, I occasionally catch a fierceness mixed with fear in another's eye that lets me know that they see me quite differently.
As someone huge.
As someone powerful.
As someone who could squelch their plans.
And there is a bulge in their right pocket that makes me suspect they've been to the wadi collecting smooth stones.

Somewhere in me now is also Goliath.

I don't like looking at the story from this lens. It is much better being David. Don't you agree?

But just as it is important for our life of faith to know and revel in our smallness, it is equally as important for our life of faith that we come to know and accept our bigness. Because that is what most of us here in this room are now most of the time: We are *big*.

We are among the most educated people on the face of the earth.
Only a quarter of Americans hold a bachelors degree.
Far fewer are able to pursue a masters degree or a doctoral degree.
We are wealthy,
at least in comparison to the vast majority of the world.
Many of us hold positions of some authority and power
or are on our way to holding them.

And the more unaware that we are of our bigness, the more likely we are to trample on others without even knowing we have done so.
Like a bull in a china shop.
Or a Goliath on a battle field.
And the more surprised we will be to come face to face–either in person or through the t.v. screen–with the angry, determined eyes of a youth who thinks that God is in *their* corner.

Who really is the "David" in today's society? It probably isn't us. And who has God on their side? Well, I'm not willing to be doctrinaire on this matter, but if the biblical witness has anything to say about it—again—we have to allow the possibility that it is not you and I.

It makes us wonder. If the key virtues of David are courage, determination, and faith, what would goodness look like in the person of Goliath? We don't get any clues from today's scripture. The original Goliath thought the gods were with him and apparently never considered the question.

But, we do get some clues from our Christian tradition—especially in person of Jesus Christ—who was the gargantuan, greatness of God poured out into a tiny human being, a descendant of David.

The Gospels tell us that he lived in solidarity with the small of the earth, taking on their concerns, bearing their trials, living their life.

The Gospels tell us he did not waste his words in trash talk to create competition, but instead used them to ask lots of hard questions,
>"If you love only those who love you, what reward will you have?"
>"Is not life more than food and the body more than clothing?"
>"Why do you see the speck in your neighbor's eye, but do not notice the log in your own?"

The Gospels tell us he was "meek and humble of heart."

And, the Gospels tell us that, like Goliath, he died, the sword of his enemy thrust into his side. But, unlike Goliath, his was a life given, not taken. And, his corpse was never food for the birds of the air and the beasts of the field. He rose from where he lay—life overturning death. Giving hope and courage to the small of the earth and a pattern of discipleship for the great who seek to stand on God's side.

May we who have been blessed so greatly in life, find a way to make our largeness largesse by walking in his footsteps.

22. *Aquinas Midday Prayer*
April 30, 2008
Acts 17:15,22–18:1

Many years ago now, when I was a college student, I came across an interview with Mother Teresa of Calcutta. The journalist was asking her about the Muslims and Hindus among whom she lived. Why hadn't she tried to convert them? Didn't it matter what religion we belong to? Shouldn't she care about their souls? Her response has always stuck with me.

She told the interviewer–in so many words–that if a person has no questions in their life, then God must be reaching them exactly where they were. If they have not the least doubt about it, then this must be the way for their salvation. But, *the moment that they had a question*, this was a grace from God, and the person was obligated to pursue that question, to search further. A question is an invitation, drawing the person on a journey closer to God. If the person doesn't pursue a question given to him, then he goes astray.

A question is a grace.

In today's reading from the book of Acts, Paul seems to have a similar insight. Paul is in Athens–the great philosophical center of the Mediterranean–and, earlier in the chapter, he is quite disgusted. He finds the people shallow and fickle, titillated by every new thought, always in search of the next intellectual or religious fad. Acts says that the city was "filled with idols"–a phrase that we should probably take quite literally, but also figuratively: The peoples' hearts belonged to many different things. They *were* the original sophists after all.

But underlying their sophistry / their fickleness, Paul senses a deep hunger – a question that is eating away at them, for which they haven't yet found an answer, no matter who they've listened to or how many conversations they've engaged. He finds this hunger symbolized in an altar he discovers dedicated "To an Unknown God."

Paul begins his preaching to this people from the space of their hunger. He names their question as a grace.

"I know about this unknown God that you've been questing after," he says. "I know the one that you've been longing for, who causes you to wonder. This God has seemed so far away, so unreachable... but actually is very near. We didn't create this God–this God has created us! This God is closer to us than our own breath!

"And now this God has called us to a new time in history. Whereas once we thought him to be unknown, now he has been made known through the words of a preacher. And we know these words are true, because this preacher was killed, but God raised him from the dead."

And some people scoffed and let the question go. But some people decided to pursue, saying "We want to hear you talk about this again." And some–like Dionysius and Damaris–became believers, because they let the question be a grace, taking them to a new place in their relationship with God.

There are two things that I think perhaps we might take from the story of Paul at Areopagus today:

The first is a deeper respect for the questions that visit us personally in our own lives. For myself, as a child, I was instructed that questions were primarily temptations of the devil–a sign of insolence, lack of faith. But, Mother Teresa and Paul alike would encourage us to look at our questions from another perspective. They are graces, inviting us to an ever deeper relationship with God and we are obligated to pursue them. Once upon a time, I thought theologians were those who had all the answers about God. Now, I know that theologians are simply those who have more questions about God than most and find their salvation in the pursuit of those questions. Honor your questions as an essential part of your spiritual journey. It's when we don't, we are in most danger of going awry.

The second challenge relates to how we will honor the questions of others, especially in our common vocation as preachers & teachers. Sometimes in our history, we have thought that the proclamation of the Gospel was to begin with the announcement of sin, pointing out where the other person was wrong, was going astray. But Mother Teresa and Paul both remind us that the best place to begin the proclamation of the Gospel is in the question. It requires finding that open space, that hunger, that vulnerability, that point of haunting wonder–indeed, the doubt– and gently naming it as grace. How would our teaching, our "homilizing," our ministry, be different if–instead of starting with what we thought people should know–we started with their questions?

The pursuit of questions is a rather scary thing. We don't quite know where we will end up when we follow them. But today's reading should give us courage. We will find the one in whom we live and breath and have our being. We will find the unknown God.

23. Opening Mass for MAPS-CGS '08 & A@H Cohort   August 22, 2008
Ezekiel 37:1-14

(This homily was preached at the conclusion of the Proseminar intensive with Scott Steinkerchner)

I know that you've been speaking with Scott this morning on the habitus of theological reflection–that practice by which we as a community seek to make connections between our faith and our lives so that the two are not separate, compartmentalized, but rather an integrated, seamless whole.

Every time that we come to this point in the liturgy, built into our Eucharistic ritual, is a moment set aside for theological reflection–a time to make connections between the readings we hear from scripture, our lives, and this liturgy that we celebrate. Usually this theological reflection has initially gone on in the study of the preacher and is polished up a bit before spoken in the midst of the assembly, but Scott asked me if perhaps I could let hang out a bit the rough meanderings of a preacher's mind so that the connection between theological reflection and preaching might be a little more transparent. How do I reflect on these readings today? It makes me a little nervous to try this way of preaching with you, but I'll give it a shot.

We've been reading from Ezekiel all week in the lectionary, and just like every other time I encounter his words, I get a bit freaked out. My first impression is that Ezekiel is one strange guy. In his call he has visions of creatures with wings and multiple faces on spinning wheels going in every direction. He eats scrolls. He can't speak. When he can he says vulgar things and does strange acts, like cutting off his hair and burning it. He reminds me a bit of some of the men–often veterans of Vietnam–that I have encountered on the streets around College Church, who are pushing shopping carts piled high with clothes and cans and singing at the top of their lungs. And I wonder in my mind, what happened to this man Ezekiel? What did he live through?

And with not too much poking around on the shelves, I can find out: he has lived through the Exile. One of the most horrific events in Israel's memory. An event that happened around 586 BC. An event that

Ezekiel's contemporaries thought could never happen. In Ezekiel's time the land that had once been a magnificent united kingdom under David, had long since been split into two kingdoms. The northern half had been conquered and decimated, but the southern half–Judah–had the temple, God's own home, and hence believed that what had happened to the north could never happen to them. Ezekiel, it turns out was a priest in that very temple, when it did happen to them.

The Babylonians from the north, under the leadership of Nebuchad-nezzar, laid siege on the city of Jerusalem. The gates were closed. Food could not come in or out. Water ran out. People starved. Parched. Until finally the walls fell. Until finally the temple fell. Until the leaders of the land, the priests of the temple were taken away in chains to another land that was not their own. A land distant from all they knew. Distant from God. Horrific as it seems, the scene that Ezekiel initially describes today in the first reading is possibly quite literal. A landscape of bones.

Who knows what kind of trauma he experienced? What Jerusalem looked like when the walls came down? When waves of the Babylonian army swept through homes of the weak and desolate with their swords and armor. What did it look like the day thereafter? The years thereafter? When Ezekiel went to sleep at night, is this the kind of scene that haunted his dreams? Did he wander through the streets of Babylon with a shopping cart?

And then in my meandering I realize that the scene he saw was not all that different than scenes our own times have witnessed. Many of these scenes have been so far from our own personal experience. We touched them only with our eyes through the T.V. screen. Pictures from Sudan. Pictures from Iraq and Afghanistan. Pictures from Rwanda. But then I begin to realize that through a vocation to ministry, you / I have touched some of what Ezekiel saw also through our ears. Listening to the veteran come back from war and his wife who doesn't know who he has become anymore. Listening to an immigrant who crossed the desert of Arizona. Listening to a prisoner in a land far from home.

And then I know that sometimes in ministry and simply in life itself, I've not only observed or heard about the land of dry bones. I've been there myself. Not in Jerusalem, but in the recesses of my mind. I remembered that the only other time I've actually had to preach on this reading from Ezekiel was right after suffering a miscarriage. And I remember how dismembered I felt after that experience, emotionally and physically scattered. And even though we don't know each other all that well at this point in the journey, I'm guessing that most of you, too, have walked quite personally through a field of bones. Most people who go into theology have. Most of us know that the shopping cart isn't that far off an option.

And then in the midst of that wondering, I hear a promise that God is going to gather up the scattered bones of the world, of our bodies, and bring them back into one. And that, as if that were not enough, God is going to breathe his own spirit into them *that might LIVE*. "I have come that you might have life and have it in abundance."

And then, in my mind, I turn and I face this table that is in front of us right now. And I ponder what it is that we think we are doing here. And I remember an ancient line from the earliest days of the church, from a book known as the Didache–the Teaching:
> "Just as the bread broken was first scattered on the hills, then was gathered and became one, so let your church be gathered from all the ends of the earth into your kingdom, for yours is glory and power through all ages."

And I begin to reflect on what Ezekiel would have us understand about this Eucharist and what this Eucharist would have us understand about Ezekiel's vision. This bread that is before us today was once scattered and dry seed. By the goodness of God and the work of human hands, it has become one bread, rattling as it came together.
> "Then the LORD said to me: Prophesy to the spirit, prophesy, son of man, and say to the spirit: Thus says the Lord God: From the four winds come, O Spirit, and breathe into these slain that they may come to life."

In a moment, we will pray the prayer of epiclesis–a prayer asking God to send down the spirit into this bread and this wine, into this space, that we may know God truly present with us. But let us remember, as the Didache states, whatever we pray for the bread and the wine, we are really praying for ourselves and our world.
> "Just as the bread broken was first scattered on the hills, then was gathered and became one, so let your church–let your people–be gathered–be raised up from all the ends of the earth and made into one. Breathe your spirit into us. Make us fully alive with your presence in the world. Bring

about through us your kingdom,... for yours is glory and power through all ages."

May the vision of Ezekiel be fulfilled in us: May we who share in this one Bread become one body, a sign of the resurrection of the world.

24. Catholic Coalition on Preaching
Morning Prayer
September 25, 2008
Acts 10:44-48

Last summer, I had the amazing privilege of spending a week in northern Montana, not far from the Canadian border on the Rocky Boy reservation. The priest on the reservation, Fr. Pete, and his Dominican sister co-worker, Sr. Kathleen Kane, had brought me out there to train local catechists—a wonderful group of women (and even one guy!) who were deeply devoted to their Catholic faith.

At night, over elk pot roast or antelope tenderloin, which Pete had shot himself, I got to have these wonderful conversations with him and Kathleen about the history of the people they serve and how they had come to be Catholic. Pete and Kathleen have lived with the Native Americans of Montana for decades and they *know* the history of the land—not just the broad sweeps of history given in text books, but the intimate memories spoken in sweat lodges and on death beds that give texture and nuance and complicate any simple tale.

They had many stories of the Church and the Indians—some predictably discouraging, some remarkably encouraging. Things that'd make you proud. Things that'd make you cringe. One story turned the history books on their heads. Fr. Pete talked about one local native population who—long before missionaries had arrived in their part of a plain—had had a vision. The elders, while praying, had seen a beautiful woman who told them to go down the Missouri River and find men in long black robes to bring back and to speak to them more about God and God's plan. This Indian nation sent a group of ambassadors by canoe down river looking for the Jesuits long before the Jesuits ever went looking for them.

I thought about these natives of the Montana plains when reflecting on today's passage from Acts about Peter and Cornelius' household.

So often, when we tell the story of Christianity in broad sweeps, we tell the story of how the apostles went out from Jerusalem after Pentecost to share the good news of Jesus' death and resurrection to the ends of the earth. The Church, set afire by God, proclaims the Word. People listen and change their lives. We baptize them. Then the Holy Spirit can come into their lives as well.

In the intimate patchwork memories of Acts, however, the storyline is a lot more messy. Peter hadn't gone seeking out Cornelius and his family. They were Gentiles, not the intended audience of the preaching mission of the early apostles who thought that the Gospel was meant only for the Jews. But, strangely, the Gentiles had come looking for Peter. After a vision from God, Cornelius sent his ambassadors out to find Peter and bring him to the family home. At Cornelius's request, Peter begins to preach, but before he is even able to finish a paragraph, the Holy Spirit bursts into the scene and gives the Gentiles the gift of tongues, like the apostles had received at Pentecost.

What is this? Everything is out of order. First you are supposed to listen. *Then* you are supposed to get baptized. *Then* you get the Holy Spirit. That's the way it is supposed to happen. Jesus said so! "Go therefore and make disciples of all nations and baptize them in the name of the Father, and the Son, and the Holy Spirit."

But then there is this God, so abundant, so full of love and excitement, so impatient to give gifts, that he can't wait for the disciples to get there. Can't even follow the order that he himself issued. Can't wait for Christmas to give the present. Jumping up and down, giggling, flapping, rips the ribbon off himself, because you just aren't unwrapping it fast enough: It's the Spirit! See, I've given you the Holy Spirit!

And, all that Peter can do really is throw up his arms. You can hear him mumbling under his breath, can't you? Basically, "Well, what the hell–I guess we better baptize them." God has raced out ahead as Peter pants to keep up.

As my colleague Scott says, "That bush was burning before we got there." Or as the Catechism of the Catholic Church (#1257) states in slightly more formal tone: "God has bound salvation to the sacrament of Baptism, but he himself is not bound by his sacraments."

As preachers, as ministers of the sacraments, I'm guessing that you already know how hard it is to have that God as a "boss." A God who puts out a handbook that says "Do it this way" but then never follows his own policies. A God who sends you on a mission and then zooms ahead and wraps it up before you get there. Your boat lands on what you believe to be virgin soil and you find God has already consummated the relationship.

And you throw up your arms and think, "Well, what the hell…
… I guess we better baptize them
… I guess we better confirm them
… I guess we better absolve them
… I guess we better anoint them
… I guess we better…O… I'll leave it there, because I'm sure you already get the point. "God has bound salvation to the sacrament of Baptism, *but he himself is not bound by his sacraments.*"

And you could get irked at God's pattern of behavior – *so* generous, *so* merciful, *so* bubbling over, *so* impatient – or you could laugh and join in the party and stay a few days.

If you've made it to this conference, I'm guessing that you're one who's learned, like Peter, just to laugh and join in the fun, because–really–is there any other God that you'd want to work for other than this one?

25. Aquinas Midday Prayer
November 19, 2008
Revelation 4:1-11

Sometimes in the various seasons of one's life, certain themes pop out. You don't intend for them to surface; it just happens that way. A couple years ago one spring it was "graffiti." We don't need to go into that now; that's for some other homily. But it just was. This fall, it has been "monastic chant." This is probably because I had the good fortune of rediscovering a lost Hildegard of Bingen CD in the trunk of my car and the privilege of visiting not one, but two monasteries in the last couple months—Gethsemani in Kentucky and St. Meinrad's in southern Indiana. Each have been very short visits, but powerfully moving, especially observing the monks at Liturgy of the Hours.

I'll be honest, the monastic life is never one that has made a lot of sense in my pragmatic German upbringing. My father, who is a very devout Catholic his whole life long and never says an unkind word about anyone, especially nuns and priests, one time admitted to me, upon having received a request for a donation from a cloistered community, "I have to say, I just don't understand that. I don't understand why they can't *do* something, can't work for a living… some sort of ministry of some kind, even if they don't earn any money. It is so utterly impractical: to lock oneself up and sing all day."

But, watching these monks in their choir stalls—standing, sometimes stooped, leaning against a cane—was strangely touching. It wasn't like they sounded good. They sounded better at Meinrad's than at Gethsemani, but not by much. They weren't particularly reverent or focused on performance. Some looked at their books, some stared at the ceiling or into space because they knew the words so well they didn't have to read any more. Day after day, month after month, year after year. The same basic simple chant with about eight notes. I kind of wondered how they kept doing it.

But in their writings, they describe what they see as the importance of what they are doing.

Browsing through the gift shop, I was particularly taken by the recorded talks of Fr. Matthew Kelty, a Cistercian, now 94, the oldest monk at Gethsemani. He says,

> "We expedite the coming [of the Kingdom of God]. Are involved in it. How? I call your attention to it. If it borders on the absurd to make cheese and cake and fudge for the Kingdom, and we do, I call your attention to what is worse than that: We sing for it.

> "This is a house of music, of song. Seven times a day we gather to sing songs. To God. To Christ. For us and for the world. For the chant has power and heals. You cannot sing to God day after day and still be governed by anger, resentment, fury, frustration or contempt. You cannot continue. You submit to healing and accept it. Chant is healing.
> And so we build the Kingdom.

> "It is coming. And we hasten the coming. We expedite it.

> "In a wild, sordid, noisy, violent world, we sing. And we sing old songs, rich in history, rooted in it, graced by God. For healing. Ours and the world's. This is the heart of Gethsemani, its point, purpose and meaning for the building of the Kingdom."

What Fr. Matthew didn't say, but I think he could, is that he and his brothers have lived their lives in one long choir practice for the Parousia, one long choir practice for the coming of the Kingdom.

I've thought about these monks frequently in recent weeks as our tiny, waxing and waning community has gathered for midday prayer. Most of us have been here long enough to remember that our worship midday was once a pretty substantive gathering, and I have wondered a bit about the worth of what we are doing. Sometimes we haven't sounded so good of late. I know yesterday I was really stretching to hit the high notes of the Justice psalm. Celeste, right next to me, was gracious enough not to hold her ears. And, last week, Rick must have had a meeting and poor Scott was the only one left to chant on this side of the chapel. It stings sometimes. And it's not particularly practical. There are lots of things waiting on our desks to be done right now, some quite urgent. People are waiting on us. Should we put important tasks for the Kingdom on hold to come and sing?

And, yet, we do. We've been doing it for all 12 years I've been here and I'm sure it goes back at Aquinas much longer than that. In fits and starts. Sometimes small; sometimes large. Sometimes on key; sometimes off. Sometimes paying attention; sometimes staring at the ceiling. Part of some greater, largely hidden effort of the Spirit perhaps to rehearse a choir for the coming Kingdom of God.

Today's reading from Revelation was written down sometime around the year 95 A.D. A time when the Christian community of Asia Minor really needed a shot in the arm. Weary and anxious, they needed to know that their efforts to live as disciples were for a purpose. They needed a sneak preview of the final production that they were rehearsing for day in and day out as Christians, at possible risk to their own lives. And of all the images that their leader, the exiled John of Patmos, might have painted to help them envision the coming Kingdom of God, he chose the image of a magnificent choir of praise—one in which all of creation was gathered around the throne of Life and Light.

It was a promise that all of the off-key tunes of their community had meaning. All of their murmuring and pitchy-ness and stretching to hit the right notes with their lives would, someday, somehow, by the grace of God be perfected and brought into a glorious harmony. And at that time, all of creation would be covered in "eyes"—inside and out, forward and backward. In essence, they would finally be able to see with clarity and insight what God was doing and had been doing all along.

And so it is with us. We sing as a little symbol of the imperfect lives we lead every day, lives that we want to make better by practice. We sing to dissolve our anger, to loosen our hurt. We sing to let go of resentment and bitterness. We sing to heal. To God. To Christ. For us and for the world. A sign of all those little efforts that we trust God will bless and harmonize, merge into one glorious song of praise.

It took me about 8 hours to prepare this humble reflection, knowing full well that it could be about an hour for each person present. I read *Sacra Pagina*. I consulted our resident New Testament exegete Sean. I visited the web site for the island of Patmos and decided to go there someday. I started writing about four different times. Along the way, I thought, "Why are you spending so much time? You're just preaching to the choir." And then I realized, "No. I'm preaching to *the choir*."

26. *Aquinas Midday Prayer*
December 3, 2008
Isaiah 25:6-10a

Those of you who were here two weeks ago today might remember that at different seasons of my life different themes seem to emerge from no where and that, during this fall semester, much of my pondering has revolved around the monastic life. In preparing for this morning, I was remembering the event earlier this September that kicked it all off. I was in Kentucky for the meeting of the Catholic Coalition on Preaching. We were in this very nice hotel in downtown Louisville, right at the corner of Fourth St. and Walnut. It was one of the busiest corners in downtown. Lots of restaurants. Lots of people. A huge flashy neon guitar hung over the street, allowing you to spot the intersection from quite a distance. And, rather hidden in the middle of it all, under a stop light, was one of those bronze plaques that marks a historical site.

Such plaques are a very dangerous thing for me. As a former history major, I experience some sort of bizarre magnetic attraction to them and have been known to hit the breaks on a highway, risking life and limb on the side of the road as eighteen-wheelers blast by to try and read them and absorb the aura of the site that they mark. This drives my son and husband nuts, but I like to try to breathe in something of the dust and see if I can imagine what happened there and be a part of it.

This plaque simply noted that it was here that Thomas Merton had had his famous "Louisville Epiphany" in 1958. It couldn't have been that famous, I thought, since I'd never heard of the Louisville Epiphany before, so fortunately the plaque continued with a long quote from Merton's work *Confessions of a Guilty Bystander:*

> "In Louisville, at the corner of Fourth and Walnut, in the center of the shopping district, I was suddenly overwhelmed with the realization that I loved all those people, that they were mine and I theirs, that we could not be alien to one another even though we were total strangers... There is no way of telling people that they are all walking around shining like the sun...

> "[I]t was as if I suddenly saw the secret beauty of their hearts, the depths of their hearts where neither sin nor desire nor self-

knowledge can reach, the core of their reality, the person that each one is in God's eyes. If only they could all see themselves as they really are....I suppose the big problem would be that we would fall down and worship each other. But this cannot be seen, only believed and 'understood' by a peculiar gift."

Now, I have stood at the bottom of a cliff in Saipan where 5000 Japanese soldiers committed *seppuku* and breathed that in. I've got a picture of myself before the plaque on the wall of St. Nazarene in Carcassonne, France where Dominic preached his Advent homilies 800 years ago. I've inhaled the smell of a 19th century homestead made of cow chips in the middle of Kansas and the ocean breezes of Umatac, Guam where Ferdinand Magellan landed when circumnavigating the globe. But what a different kind of experience it was to try to breathe in the essence of 4th and Walnut.

It wasn't the sense of trying to enter into the past to imagine what *had* happened there so much as trying to totally enter into the present and see what was *still* happening there, if one but had the eyes to see it. It was a place in which to penetrate not so much the mystery of time as the mystery of timelessness. To see reality clearly. To see what really, really is... to see with God's eyes. As Merton notes, to be able to absorb the true essence of a place like 4th and Walnut is a "peculiar gift" indeed.

This is the gift that Isaiah seems to have received so long ago in Jerusalem. The time in which "first Isaiah" lived was not a glorious time in Israel's history. The kingdom that had once been united by David and Solomon had divided and fallen into disrepair. It suffered poor leadership, corruption, decay–all the ordinary struggles every nation seems to face perennially. And yet Isaiah stands at the corner of 4th and Walnut in downtown Jerusalem and sees God hanging the lights for a great festival, sees the LORD setting a table, conversing with the wine sommelier .

"On *this* mountain the LORD of hosts will provide for all people a rich feast..." says Isaiah, "On *this* mountain the veil that hides things–that deceives us–all falls away. We are finally going to be able to see things as they really are. On *this* mountain, at *this* intersection, God is alive and active. God is doing something. Do you see it?... And, can you speak about it?".... *How do you go about telling people that they are shining like the sun?*

And if we fling these doors open *(open chapel doors)* and peer, as if from a window, from this space into the corner of 4th and Walnut here at Aquinas, what is going on out there…. *Really, really.* What if we could see like Isaiah saw? Like Merton saw? Like God sees? Would we see rays coming from Paula's desk… a glow emanating from Janel's office? Who is in our kitchen and what is cooking? Are there linens being snapped? Bouquets being trimmed? Is light from the basement eeking out through the floorboards? Is that what we should/could/would be seeing… if we should /could/would really see? *(long pause for looking)*

We have now entered into the season of Advent, a time of preparation for the feast. Let us spend some time practicing to *see*–to really *see*–with the prophets and monks. And not be afraid to tell a few people what God is doing here… to tell them that they are shining like the sun.

27. Aquinas Midday Prayer
Feast of St. Catherine of Siena
April 29, 2009

(The reading for this preaching was the same as the one I used for the feast of Catherine in 2002, p. 35)

When I was growing up, I was deeply enamored with the orange St. Joseph edition of *Catholic Saints for Boys and Girls.* I used to spend hours pouring over the drawings of these holy men and women. There were lots of Catherines in there and they could be hard to keep straight. I remember Catherine of Siena stood out because she was always depicted carrying a boat. I wondered what this was all about. I'd met people who walked around with a *chip* on their shoulder, but never anyone with a *ship* on their shoulder.

Alas, I was not curious enough to find out because I was much too preoccupied trying to re-create a habit for myself in the style of Catherine Laboure–an endeavor which met an abrupt end when my mother went into the hall closet and shrieked, *"What has happened to all my hangers? Why are they all bent out of shape?"*

Perhaps this should have immediately shifted my interests more toward Catherine of Siena, but that did not really happen until I came to Aquinas under what was then known as the Catherine of Siena scholarship. I figured that if this woman was somehow responsible for helping to fund my education, I should get to know her somehow and we should be friends.

But this was harder to do than it looked.

I did a paper on her once. Then in history of preaching, I even did a huge major project–reading her letters and her *Dialogues.* The more I learned, the less we connected.

She was Italian…effusive, emotive–in ways that we Germans just don't feel very comfortable with. (On principle, I try not to cry more than once a year.)

She writes about fire and sweetness, devils and blood. I write about demographic shifts in U.S. Catholicism and conflict management.

Still we tried to reach out for one another.

Visiting Avignon, I was stunned by the immensity of the papal palace she walked up to. Got a sense of how small she must have felt requesting an audience with the pope, but had a hard time visualizing that conversation.

I dragged my son to St. Maria Sopra Minerva in Rome where I sat on the ground next to her tomb for quite a while and tried to feel some real connection with her–until Micah finally gave me an elbow and pointed to the line that was forming, saying, *"Mom, you are hogging the saint."*

Yes, it has been an uneasy relationship, but we talk. I tell her I think she is a little crazy and that she should eat more.

And she tells me that I should be more courageous and adventuresome in my relationship with God.

And, I tell her to strive for some balance and pace herself for the long haul.

And, she's made clear that I should be doing more hands on work in the area of justice for the poor.

And we might be like ships passing in the night… except that both of us are on the same ship, and perhaps even more so, under that same ship.. And maybe that is where you've met Catherine, too.

For a long time, I'd assumed that the ship in Catherine's picture was an iconographer's invention–a symbol of the role Catherine had played in steering the Church thru the Avignon papacy. In truth, it was not an artist's creation, but one deeply rooted in Catherine's own imagination–based on an event which took place shortly before the letter we read today was written.

The event took place in 1380–a time that found Catherine in Rome advocating for the new pope Urban, hopeful that reform was eminent, worried that it was not. She spent *her* days hogging the tomb of St. Peter, fixated on Giotto's mosaic of the apostle's humble fishing vessel.

One Sunday, during Vespers, Catherine watched as the bark left the mosaic and came to rest squarely on her shoulders. Her companions saw nothing, but witnessed the fragile, thin Catherine collapse to the ground as if crushed by a great weight. She was paralyzed and had to be carried home. She never recovered and, three months later, died.

Our own stories might not be so dramatic or visceral. Publicly, we might not even admit that we have any clue what Catherine experienced. Except that in the dark, at four in the morning, lying in bed at the end of the semester, with "to do" lists running through our minds like the constant streaming text on the bottom of the CNN screen, worried about this parishioner and that co-worker, pondering the meaning of this theological trend and that papal pronouncement, agonizing over next year's budget and this week's hire, Catherine sneaks up on us and whispers whatever the Italian equivalent is of "*Pot calling kettle black.*"

And she says, "It's heavy isn't it?"
And slightly panicked, gasping for air, you say, "Yes."
Pause.
"Crushing actually."
"I know."

"But I love this ship."
"I know."

"But I think it might end up killing me."
"I know."

"But I wouldn't choose any life other than this one. My whole heart belongs to the Church. If I had a thousand lives, they'd all belong to this people. If I had a thousand wishes, I'd give them all on their behalf... Pour out my heart over the Church, Lord."
"Amen. Deo gratias, Amen. Gesu dolce, Gesu amore. Amen."

Long pause.
"You know I don't want to be like you when I grow up. I think you are weird."
"I know."

"Don't leave. Stay right here beside me, okay?"
"I will," she says.

28. Aquinas Midday Prayer
Feast of St. Thecla
September 23, 2009

A reading from the Acts of Paul and Thecla (#26-35)

And Thecla said unto Paul: I will cut my hair round about and follow thee whithersoever thou goest. But he said: The time is ill-favoured and thou art comely: beware lest another temptation take thee, worse than the first, and thou endure it not but play the coward. And Thecla said: Only give me the seal in Christ, and temptation shall not touch me. And Paul said: Have patience, Thecla, and thou shalt receive the water.

And Paul sent away Onesiphorus with all his house unto Iconium, and so took Thecla and entered into Antioch: and as they entered in, a certain Syriarch, Alexander by name, saw Thecla and was enamoured of her, and would have bribed Paul with money and gifts. But Paul said: I know not the woman of whom thou speakest, neither is she mine. But as [Alexander] was of great power, he himself embraced her in the highway; and she endured it not, but sought after Paul and cried out bitterly, saying: Force not the stranger, force not the handmaid of God.

...

But [Alexander] ...being ashamed of what had befallen him, brought her before the governor; and when she confessed that she had done this, he condemned her to the beasts...

Now when the beasts were led in procession, they bound her to a fierce lioness... but the lioness, when Thecla was set upon her, licked her feet, and all the people marvelled....

Then did they put in many beasts, while she stood and stretched out her hands and prayed. And when she had ended her prayer, she turned and saw a great tank full of water, and said: Now is it time that I should wash myself. And she cast herself in, saying: *In the name of Jesus Christ do I baptize myself on the last day.* And all the women seeing it and all the people wept, saying: Cast not thyself into the water: so that even the governor wept that so great beauty should be devoured by seals. So, then, she cast herself into the water in the name of Jesus Christ; and the seals, seeing the light of a flash of fire, floated dead on the top of the water. And there was about her a cloud of fire, so that neither did the beasts touch her, nor was she seen to be naked.

Now the women, when other more fearful beasts were put in, shrieked aloud, and some cast leaves, and others nard, others cassia, and some balsam, so that there was a multitude of odours; and all the beasts that were struck thereby were held as it were in sleep and touched her not; so that Alexander said to the governor: I have some bulls exceeding fearful, let us bind the criminal to them. And the governor frowning, allowed it, saying: Do that thou wilt. And they bound her by the feet between the bulls, and put hot irons under their bellies that they might be the more enraged and kill her. They then leaped forward; but the flame that burned about her, burned through the ropes, and she was as one not bound."

Preaching:

I had another reflection planned for today. It was about Germany and history and the prophet Ezra who appears in the 1st reading from the lectionary. It was a pretty good reflection and it was two thirds written. Someday it might make a reappearance. But then there was this woman nagging at the back of my mind. She has almost been forgotten in the shadows of history. Indeed maybe she is apocryphal, like St. Christopher or Juan Diego. She is surely ancient, from another distant time. Yet she kept knocking and crying out with a faint voice, "Hello, it is my feast day today. Remember me?" This woman's name is Thecla.

All that we know of her comes from a second century work called the *Acts of Paul and Thecla*, written perhaps somewhere around 160 A.D., and commented on by Tertullian. She is remembered as a young woman from Iconium who was absolutely enchanted with Paul's preaching. As she listened to him speak about celibacy, she saw options for herself as a woman that she'd never imagined before. She broke off her engagement and decided to follow Paul. This did not go over well with her family or her fiancé who turned her over to the governor. The governor had Paul beaten and then thrown out of the city. Thecla he decided to have burned so as to discourage other women from following her example. But the flames would not touch her and she set out to find Paul again.

Turns out Paul was not particularly keen on having this woman stalking him, insisting on being included. He wants her to wait, wants to delay her baptism. But she doesn't let up.

In the passage we read, another man falls in love with Thecla and, like a bad dream that keep repeating itself, Thecla once again refuses him and is sent to the governor and condemned to death. This time beasts are let into the arena, but refuse to eat her. And Thecla has had enough. If after two near-martyrdom experiences still no one will baptize her, well, she will just have to do it herself.

"In the name of Jesus Christ," she says, diving into a tank of water, "I baptize myself."

The power of her splash instantly kills all the seals in the tank.

One last time, they try to do away with her, tying her between bulls, but the cords that held her deteriorate in flame. They turn to ash at her feet. The last line of the reading is my favorite: "she was as one not bound."

She was as one not bound.

In a church that has done a very good job at teaching me the virtue of patience, Thecla reminds me that there is also such a thing as holy impatience.

Now this is a dangerous virtue because it can so easily be abused. We should consider it in the same way that we consider the holy anger Jesus exercised in the cleansing of the temple. He didn't walk around knocking pigeons off tables every day, but sometimes the situation calls for it. The key is to know when.

Sometimes in our interactions with each other, we can get stuck in a state of impasse without even realizing it. We get locked into the dynamics of struggle and see no way out.

Someone says to us: "This is good and beautiful." And we say, "I would like it." And the other says, "Ask me to give it to you." "Okay, can I please have it?" "No" "Why not?" "Because." "Please." "No." "Please." "No."

Or maybe it goes a little like this. "You can't do this." "O, yes, I can." "No, you can't." "Watch me, I can." "No, that's not right." "What's wrong with the way I'm doing it?" "You are doing it wrong." "Well, you show me how to do it then." "No, I won't."

We get stuck in tug-of-war situations that are tremendously draining. The other side is pulling as hard as it can. We are pulling as hard as we can. And if you ask why, each would say, "I have to do this or I'll end up in the mud pit," forgetting that there is another option, which is to say, "I'm just not interested in playing this game any more"—a response that would also leave the other side reeling.

And she was as one unbound.

When Micah was about four or so, I remember coming to my mom's house to pick him up after classes and she alerted me that Micah had gotten into a fight with Mary Kate–age five, another child my mom babysat–and bitten her, and my mom thought I should handle it. I said to Micah, "Tell me about biting Mary Kate." It turned out that she'd wanted to play house and he didn't want to play house. She blocked the door with her body so that he couldn't leave, and so he bit her. I told Micah that biting was wrong and that I wanted him to sit in the room and think about another way that he could have gotten out of this situation. Of course I intended him to say something about how he could have used words rather than teeth–you know, along that line. Ten minutes later Micah came out with a piece of paper on which he had drawn a map of the room. "See," he said, "This is a window. Next time I will go out the window."

Scripture says that there is a time for everything under the sun. A time to wait and a time to act. A time to submit and a time to refuse. A time to play it safe and a time to break free. A time to use the door and a time to use the window. Holy impatience.

And perhaps this is why Thecla has come knocking at our door today. Because maybe there are some games we don't have to play. Maybe there are some battles we just don't have to fight. Maybe there's permission we don't have to ask. Maybe we just dive into the water.

She was as one not bound.

And I see Rosa Parks plopping down in the front of the bus.
And I hear President Obama saying, "Yeah, I'm just not going to do that race card conversation any more."

She was as one not bound.

And I hear women turning fifty, and seventy, and seventy-five saying, "You know I just don't have time for this stuff anymore."

And I meet pastors who say, "I'm just not waiting for an answer anymore."

She was as one not bound.

And I see Israel standing up, "Yeah, I'm not doing the brick-making thing anymore."

And I hear Mary singing the Magnificat through the hills of Judea, that the "powerful" aren't really in power anymore.

And I see Lazarus being unwrapped, because death doesn't rule anymore.

And I listen to Jesus cracking out of the tomb on Easter morn, because there is a Kingdom to be preached and he just doesn't have time to chat with the stone blocking the entrance anymore.

She was as one not bound.

Holy impatience. Use it wisely.

29. *Aquinas Midday Prayer*
October 21, 2009
Romans 6: 12-18

Several years back PBS hosted a renowned documentary series on the Civil War, and then also that period of US history known as the Reconstruction. Of course, a climax in the midst of the saga was the Emancipation Proclamation–Lincoln's announcement that the Southern slaves were now free. It was a momentous event in our country's history–a real turning point, especially in the African-American story.

But as the subsequent episodes explained, freedom wasn't exactly all that it was cracked up to be. While many slaves did take off from the plantations and start a new life, many others stayed put, and not much changed in their lives at all. *They were free.* The shackles unlocked. But how to claim that freedom? How to live like free people? That was a different matter.

Turns out that one of the cruelest things about slavery is not what it does to the human body–terrible as that surely is–but what it does to the human imagination. The way that it darkens dreams. Boxes in possibilities. Trains the mind not to see them any more, not to test them any more.

The antithesis of a "gift that keeps giving," slavery is a "robbery that keeps robbing."

Today, the lectionary hands us a passage from the Letter to the Romans on the topic of sin. I find it interesting that of all the images that Paul could use to describe the effect of sin in our lives, the image he chooses is that of slavery.

Even though slavery in Paul's time was somewhat different than slavery in our own nation's history, it remains a provocative image. We've heard lots of sermons on sin; the Romans probably did, too. And, perhaps we've grown quite blasé about it. So Paul uses the strongest language he's got.

Sin, in Paul's mind, is a relentless master–
controlling,

forcing,
manipulating.
It consumes the human body and transforms it into a weapon. Making it do things it doesn't really want to do.

But *worse* than that—yes, *worse* than that – it infects the imagination,
so that even when one has been set free from this tyrant...
even when Jesus Christ has died and risen and defeated this evil once and for all...
even when God has pronounced the Emancipation Proclamation over the human race....
We find ourselves strangely immobile, stuck in place.

And that is the reality that so puzzles and frustrates Paul in today's reading: How could these people who have walked through the waters of baptism, who have died and risen with Christ, still live remarkably as they did before? Yes, sin is a hideous thing, indeed!
And this "Emancipation-thing" doesn't quite fix everything the way that we thought that it might.

Believe it or not, I've actually pondered variations
on Paul's quandary a lot.
I imagine you have to. Questions like:

Why does God even permit sin?
And why does God allow it to have *such* powerful effects?
Like really terrible things happening to innocent bystanders?
And why, if Baptism is supposed to wash away sin, can't you see it consistently and markedly in the lives of the baptized?

And why does this salvation thing seem like an aborted rescue operation—where God swooshes in and blasts open the cell door and clips the chains, unties the prisoner, but then sort of vacates the scene?

Why doesn't God *make* us to run, make us to follow?
Why doesn't God *make* us do what is right?
Just pick us up and carry us out to a safe, happy zone?
What good was the Emancipation in the first place?

And pondering these questions has led me to observe that, quite possibly, of all the things that God values—
and I mean of ALL the things God values—

God apparently values human freedom / human agency *most highly of all.*

That unlike the relentless master known as sin,
God refuses to coerce, to push or to limit–even when it might seem to be in our best interest.
God leaves humans completely and radically free.

And why?
I think this may have something to do with the nature of God as love.
St. John makes this claim in the letter right down the Table of Contents from Paul's: God is love. It's not just one of God's many attributes.
No, God *IS* love.
And love, by its very definition, requires free response.
I can't *make* you like me.
I can't *force* you to love me.
It sounds wrong to the ear, doesn't it? Like words that just can't be put next to each other in the same sentence. Force and love are like repelling magnets.

God loves us, and God's deepest desire is that we might love in return. As Jesus says at the Last Supper: *I* call you friends. I want nothing more than to be in relationship. To be in covenant. But in order for it really to be friendship, you must be truly free. And that part, I can't *make* happen.

Pure love requires pure freedom.

And if this doesn't frighten the bejeebers out of you then I haven't said well what I think St. Paul wants us to know:

That we have a real freedom to say "no" as well as to say "yes."
We have a real freedom to choose death as well as choose life.
We have a real freedom to sin as well as to love. We have a real freedom to set down stakes in the land of sin,
> to lie and abuse,
> to slaughter and avenge,
> to blow the whole world up if we want to, and God isn't going to do anything to stop it.

But if this doesn't thrill you, then I also haven't said well what I think St. Paul wants us to know:

That our choices are real and do make a difference.
That we are not slaves of sin any longer and *don't have to live in that land.*
That we can say "YES" and not just "no."
That we can shout "LIFE" and not just "death."
That we can choose LOVE and not just sin.
That we have a real freedom, in Paul's words,
to "present ourselves to God as raised from the dead to life"
and know that we will be embraced with wide open arms.
Thank God.

Thank God.

That's where St. Paul ends the passage: Thank God.

You've been freed FROM sin; freed FOR friendship with God.

And *you know that*, St. Paul says.

The teaching you've received has patterned your hearts to beat to this rhythm.

You know it, so pull out those stakes and let's move on toward the Promised Land.

30. *Aquinas Midday Prayer*
February 18, 2010
Deuteronomy 30:15-20 & Luke 9

For years now I have been on the bandwagon of clear communication. First as a writing teacher, now as a homiletics instructor and difficult conversations devotee, there are few things that irk me more than mixed messages. A few years ago, on NPR I heard a newspaper editor bemoaning the muddy mess of facts that one of the reporters had turned in, "That's not right," he said, "that's not even wrong!" A number of us here have probably tried to grade a paper or two like that in our lifetimes. Mixed messages. Muddied messages. Even contradictory messages.

Today's lectionary readings seem to present us with such a puzzlement. In the first reading from Deuteronomy, we hear, loud and clear: "I have set before you life and death, blessing and curse. Choose life then that you and your descendants might live." Then, in the Gospel, we hear, "Pick up your cross and follow me. For whoever wishes to save his life will lose it." Choose life. Pick up the cross. Choose life. Pick up the cross.

Here we stand at the start of what many think of as ecclesial New Year's ready to make our resolutions. So which is it, Good God?

Choose life. Pick up the cross. Make up your mind.

And then from way down deep, comes a not-very-pretty story from my own past. Indeed it so nearly went awry that it frightens me still to speak it out loud. It was early fall of 1994. I was newly married. I was teaching at a brand new school. I was nervous. I was nauseous. I was late, still late... still late. Ah, yes, of course, I was pregnant. My parents had always made each new pregnancy seem like such a wonderful thing, but this one did not feel that way at all and I didn't know what do to with that. I was so sick to my stomach I couldn't get out of bed and used up all my sick days.

But worse than that, I became depressed. Like pull down the shades and hide under the covers depressed. Like dull numbness, can't-feel-anything, don't-want-to-go-on depressed. And the friends of Job began to show up at my bedside and say things like, "You've done your best, but maybe the timing just isn't right.... God couldn't fault you. Maybe it is time to end this." And this is the part that scares me the most–that I entertained that thought long and hard for about 24 hrs. And, honestly, if it were not for the absolutely unambiguous, consistent clarity of my parents from the day of my birth that abortion is wrong, I do not know if I would have had sufficient wherewithal in my very fuzzy, chaotic mind to make a good choice.

But, I said, "No, I can't do that."

And my husband pulled back the covers and said, "Okay, then you need to get out of bed."

And, in that moment, choosing life and picking up the cross–two options that seem so diametrically opposed–merged into one mystery.

Most of you probably haven't encountered that mystery quite so *literally* in a pregnancy, but I have no doubt that you know exactly what I mean: That there are times in each of our lives when choosing to do what is right requires tremendous personal sacrifice yet simultaneously touches what is deepest and truest and most real and ultimately bears life within ourselves and for others.

Times when Christ's promise of abundant life feels an awful lot like losing the one you have and at the bottom of the gut you discover the courage to do it anyway. And in the history of the Church this mystery has a name: the Paschal Mystery–pick up your cross and choose life.

The danger is that this conversation could go south really fast and it often has. Sometimes we have wielded this mystery like it was a magic wand: *"Hey you over there–transformative suffering, now!"*

We've judged those who don't suffer in the spirit that we think they ought. We've named peoples' crosses for them. We've told them which sufferings were their lot in life that they ought to bear. And we've condemned those who couldn't crawl out of bed and who made bad choices.

And in doing so, we've often overlooked perhaps the most critical word in the paschal formula of "pick up your cross and choose life" which I think is the word "choose."

There is a terrible amount of suffering in the world and morning sickness and depression are just the edge of it. There is cancer and there is Alzheimer's. There is child abuse and there is rape. There is domestic violence and alcoholism. There is divorce and there is rage. Earthquakes and mud slides, floods and foreclosures. And while we acknowledge that God permits it, we wouldn't say God desires it / wills it. None of it is caused by God. None of it *is* of God. And none of it is inherently redemptive.

Some people will suffer tragedies their whole life long and never find any good in any of it because *there is no good in suffering.* They will not become more human through it; indeed their humanity will be diminished by it. *Suffering in itself is not redemptive.*

Suffering only becomes redemptive when choice is involved. When the human person, through the goodness of God, is able to choose how they are going to respond to the suffering.

When instead of becoming bitter or shriveled, the human instead allows the suffering to make them more empathetic.

When instead of retreating into isolation, the human decides to reach out to others.

When instead of allowing suffering to make one opaque, guarded, protected; the human allows suffering to make one transparent, even translucent.

God is not in the great wind, the earthquake, the fire.
And, God is not in the cross.
God is in the still small voice.
God is in the choice.
God is in the one who decided not to flee but to hang there.

I remember one day climbing back into the car, having just vomited on the side of the road, shaking, with grass stains on my knees and Mike handing me a McDonald's napkin from the glove compartment. And I said, "Someday we are going to look at this child and say that this was the best thing to ever happen in our lives." And we both started laughing and laughing because the idea was just so preposterous.

But since meeting Micah, not one day has gone by in which I did not think that very thought. Watching the Olympics last night with his teenage head on my shoulder, I remembered again that virtually everything that gives me joy in life right now (even beyond his presence)–the decision to come to Aquinas, my passion for Catechesis of the Good Shepherd, living where I live–all of it happened because he came into our life and because God helped us to choose to receive him as gift.

And realizing that, it strikes me that the proper response to Paschal Mystery is not to exhort that it happen where it is not, but to celebrate that it happens when it does. To celebrate the goodness of a God who, in every age and place, still stirs the human spirit to embrace life in the midst of suffering.

In the Haitian who begins to rebuild.

In the woman who screws up the courage to leave that abusive husband once and for all.

In the religious who struggles to be faithful to vows made with zealous naiveté so long ago.

In every mother who crawls out of bed.

And ultimately, in Jesus Christ who laid down his life so he could take it up again.

Every Mass, all year long we say is a celebration of this Paschal Mystery, but there is a most particular way in which the season of Lent calls us to choose to invite God into the space of our suffering–whatever that suffering might be right–and transform it that it might become redemptive.

In this holy season, let us celebrate and welcome God into our still small choices.

31. Aquinas Midday Prayer
September 1, 2010
1 Corinthians 3:1-9

So I was sitting on the floor in the stacks of the library yesterday morning checking out the commentaries on Corinthians when Chloe saddled up next to me and whispered in my ear: "So I hear you are looking for the dirt on the Paul and Apollos affair."

"It's true," I said, "You know I don't like preaching on the letters of Paul–often I just don't find he makes much sense. If he was taking Proseminar, I would ding him on use of punctuation and run on sentences."

"Well you know, the habitus of communication *was* a big part of the problem here," she said.

"No kidding."

"Yep. Paul was an amazing man, full of zeal for Christ, able to endure any hardship for the cause of the Gospel. You name it, he persevered through it. But if you have a hard time reading him, you should have tried to listen to him preach."

"I've heard he was not all that much to look at and not all that interesting to listen to."

"Remember that kid who fell out of the window in Acts?"

"I do. I do. He could be a bit long-winded, no?"

"Well, it doesn't mean that we didn't love or appreciate him. After all, he was the founder of our community at Corinth. He was like a father to us.... To me. He was the one through whom we first heard about Jesus, about his death and resurrection, and the wisdom of God present in weakness. He was our patron before God, and the larger Church. He was the one who appointed me to lead the community and to be his eyes and ears. No, we owed a great deal to him."

"So tell me about Apollos."

"Eyeyeye. Now, he *was* something to look at... and better yet to *hear*. A real feast for the ear. Wow. Talk about gifted. You know those preachers that you could listen to for hours? The words that rolled off Apollos' lips tasted like honey. When he spoke the birds paused mid-flight and just circled. Children stopped their play and sat at his feet. Strangers would gather at the edges of the circle, intrigued by his voice and find themselves magnetically drawn in to find out more. He, too, became like a patron of our community, helping to connect us with God and a wider network of Christians."

"So what happened next?" I asked.

"Read the text closely," she admonished.

"We do that here," I nodded. "We try to make a practice of it."

"Well, look between the lines and you'll see there was great tension in the community. Some thinking we should structure our community around Paul's patronage, some around Apollos'... others reminding us that it was Jesus we really belonged to. Like Christianity was some kind of competition. Silliness really, but a dangerous silliness."

"Who's fault was it?" I queried.

"No one's really... and everyone's. I mean no one was intending to cause a brouhaha. No one was intending to divide the community. Apollos never meant to become Paul's rival. Paul never meant to become Apollos' adversary. But there were little things that they weren't attentive to that made things worse. Paul not quite knowing what to do with a dazzling newcomer who arrived in his absence. Apollos not being very astute as to the way Paul might feel about his presence. A community less mature in its handling of things than it would like to think. And then there was a contributing factor that no one really thought much about at all."

Intrigued, I pressed on: "What was that?"

"The system... the way both Paul and Apollos had set things up. When they sought to build up the Christian community at Corinth, they simply borrowed from what they'd seen in the culture. All over the Mediterranean world, we had a system of patron/client relationships.

Both of them just assumed our community would be set up on that model. What they didn't see was that this kind of model is a breeding ground for competitiveness. There can only be one person at the top. In order to get what they need the people need to be loyal to their patron and divide themselves against one another."

"Huh. That must have really been a problem."

"It was. Sometimes it is the hidden things that no one is looking at that are at the root of it all. Not everyone can spot those."

"We call that practice 'analysis of social context,'" I proudly informed her. "We work really hard here at trying to cultivate attention to the underlying cultural presuppositions that influence so many things. But it is really hard to make this a habit. How did you bring this insight to light?"

"Well, I wrote Paul about it. I said, 'Hey, look at what is going on here. It's silly, but dangerous silly. I'm wondering if we should think about being Church in another way. Maybe modeling ourselves after organizations in the business world or in politics isn't really the way to go. Maybe we could dream up another way of being community, give ourselves a new metaphor to consider.

'Like a body?' Paul suggested.

'Yes, like a body with many parts,' I affirmed, 'Or like a farm with many hands.'

'Like where one person sows, and another person waters?'

'Yes, but God makes it grow,' I added.

'Totally,' he said. 'God makes it grow. That is what we've so often forgotten. God is the one who is ultimately in charge. God makes it grow.'"

"We call that 'collaboration,'" I boasted. "It's a central commitment of our school."

"No kidding," she said. "Is it true you've taken Paul's epistle so seriously? How's that working out for you?"

I turned my head and looked out at the small scattering of people spread out across the library, religious and lay, studying side by side in the midst of these stacks, though not quite knowing each other yet. And I heard laughter coming from Rm. 225 where colleagues–women and men–were plotting committee agendas. As my eyes reached the windows, my mind began to meander farther–to times around the lunch table and around the chapter room table and here around this altar table. Some funny and light-hearted. Some unspeakably painful and divisive, hurtful down to the bones. Some serious and profoundly moving. And I thought of these episodes multiplied a hundred times over in the parish where I spend my Sundays. And our diocese. And even beyond.

For some reason I found myself thinking about the document *Co-workers in the Vineyard* ,which the USCCB put out a few years back – a document for which I was privileged to participate in some committee work that led to Chapter 3. I remembered how the National Association for Lay Ministry, with eager anticipation, had named its annual conference after the document, trusting that it would be passed by the date of the conference. And I remembered the rocky road that the document encountered at the bishops' gathering when several bishops had questioned the very use of the term "ministry" alongside the word "laity." And Bishop Kicanas of Tucson told us they almost thought they were going to have to change the name of the conference to *"Undocumented Co-workers in the Vineyard."* But then Cardinal Avery Dulles had stood up and said, basically, 'Stop the silliness. Dangerous silliness."

And with this thought, I remembered Chloe was still there. And I turned back to her with a smile, "I think we are still trying to figure it out... but maybe we are making progress. How did it work for you all in Corinth?"

Chloe in turn gazed out the window with a far off look in her eye. And I wish I could have read what was going through her mind. What had ever become of Apollos and Paul? Did she bear memories of a painful distancing between the two great, gifted men as many scripture scholars believe occurred? Or–as suggested in the pastoral epistles–had they become real colleagues with one another in ministry, to such a degree that Paul advocated on Apollos' behalf to Titus, encouraging him to equip Apollos and his friend Zenas on another preaching journey? Or, even better yet, is it possible that Paul's letter helped to heal the divisions in that community and that, at a later date, as St. Jerome attested, Apollos returned to Corinth to become its bishop?

I don't know. In the end she didn't say. She shrugged and smiled, "'God chooses the foolish of the world to shame the wise, and God chooses the weak of the world to shame the strong…so that no human being might boast before God.' (1 Cor 1:27-29) In the end, it is just important to keep trying."

There was a long pause. "Do you have any more of these practices—or habits—as a community?" she asked.

"Believe it or not, yes, we do. One more. It's called theological reflection… a fancy name for fostering connections between the faith that has been passed onto us by our ancestors and the life we lead as Christians today."

"Wow," she admitted, "that sounds really challenging. Sounds like it would require listening really hard to voices that are sometimes hard to hear in today's world. But what a difference it could make."

"True." I had to confess. "So true."

32. *Aquinas Institute Midday Prayer*
On the departure of Celeste
December 15, 2010
Luke 7:18b-23

I feel the need to admit that I started on this reflection eight times over, each time with far too much in mind, complicated and convoluted. What to say on an occasion like this, after a semester like this, in the richness of a season like this one?

Perhaps it is best just to start where the Gospel starts: There were two seekers sent by John on a journey to Jesus, to find out if he was the real thing. They were in the pursuit of truth, we might say — a knowledge, an insight that would make all their waiting and searching in life have meaning. "Are you the One the prophets foretold? The one who will usher in the Kingdom of God? Or should we go on looking for another?"

It's a quest that we know here all too well, no? "Veritas" emblazoned across our school shield. It's what drew many of us to the study of theology. We want to know what is true. It makes us ravenously hungry in a way that nothing else does.

A few years ago, you might remember, a group of us got so obsessed with the question of truth and how we might know it that we locked ourselves up in the Love Shack for 13 hours straight, basically forgetting to eat or take bathroom breaks.

I think it is safe to say we can embrace these two disciples as "our people," as Seán might say.

What's interesting in this Gospel passage is Jesus' response to their quest. Note he doesn't give them the straight up, simple answer to the question they are asking. Instead he shifts the seekers gaze to the world around them and says "Go back and tell John what you see and hear."

Luke doesn't insert a pause button in the narrative here, but I tend to think there was one. A still moment in time where the two woke up to where they were and the multitudes that surrounded them and just looked around.

It's a critical moment in the truth-seeker's journey to become aware of their senses. To use the eyes. To open the ears. To smell the smells and taste the tastes. There is a big huge world out there, flush with data that overwhelms what any one person can absorb.

And that is what makes this step in the story so very challenging. For we can see and hear SO many things.

The critical verb I hear in this phrase is "tell." You must not hold all these perceptions to yourself. You need to find the courageous voice to speak. And it is true that you might not have the whole picture, and it is true that you might see things you'd rather not say, and it is true that it'd be easier to just keep certain thoughts to yourself, but I want you to lay your cards on the table. Tell what you see. Tell what you hear.

When I think back to our thirteen hour conversation, this is the part that I remember most. The intentional effort to speak what we had seen and we had heard in our lives, even though it might sound a little goofy, even though it might be challenged and critiqued, even though it sounded flimsy and impossible when we laid it out there, and we might be laughed at or shown the error of our perceptions.

Say it as you see it. Say it as you hear it.

In the Gospel, Jesus then helps the two to decipher what they are seeing and hearing, to winnow through the massiveness of their observing and pull out certain essential facets of it. He connects what they are seeing to the words of the prophets about what God's Reign looks like.

He points left to a man whose hands are caressing over and over again the face of his wife, and says: "The blind see." He points to the right, to an elderly woman hobbling along with the assistance of a dear friend and says: "The lame walk." He walks a little further and nods toward two outcasts hugging one another: "The lepers are cleansed."

And the walk goes on, all through the market, as Jesus let's them know what he sees and what he hears when he looks around him. Until Jesus finally says: "Blessed is the one who takes no offense in me."

117

It is kind of a funky line, very intriguing. For here is the strangest grace discovered in the truth seeker's journey–a grace many of us have known. Our need for the clear, definitive, simple answer we thought we were looking for fades, and instead we are left with a relationship, in which each person is free to be herself/himself and offense is no longer taken.

It is difficult to describe the sacredness of this moment of realization. The awareness that, even though we were no closer to seeing the same thing and hearing the same voices, it didn't bug us any more. I remember sitting across the dining room table from Dominic and saying, "You have challenged my ideas constantly for years now, never letting anything rest. I have always thought this meant you thought me foolish, but for you, it is a sign that you find me a worthy opponent, isn't it?" And he nodded his curt Dominic nod. And the offense was gone.

To this day, I allow Celeste to say things to me that no one else would be able to get away with, and I suspect the reverse is true. Two weeks ago, when I sent an email to her past colleagues inviting them to send a note to put in her book, Dominic and Scott both quickly wrote long letters back, which–if you've ever tried to conduct email correspondence with either of them–you know is saying something. Truth binds us to one another in ways we never imagined.

In my mind, I've come to think of these two disciples on journey as the earliest prototypes of the Dominican life. And the experiences they shared with Christ give us clues to a fulsome spirituality for a Dominican institution–a spirituality devoted to three main practices, none of which can really be engaged without the others:

Pursuing truth
Speaking truthfully
Being true to one another.

Today we come to the end of a very difficult semester in which we have had to let go of a lot: Mary, Kathy, Kate, Janel, and now Celeste. Many questions have ricocheted through these halls: "What is going on? Why is she going? Am I safe? Is the school going to survive? What is true? Have I found what I am looking for or should I search for another?" It has been a frightening and unsettling time and it still is.

When I look outside my window each morning I can see an old tree across the alley. At this time of year, when all the leaves are gone, I can see the naked trunk with its jumble of branches and limbs and everything is visible. And it is starkly clear where the storms of the past year and tree trimmers have taken off some pretty significant branches. Whether it will emerge again in the spring is always a mystery to me. I am not a botanist (really my science knowledge is incredibly weak) but I always picture that the life of the tree in winter is going down into its roots and finding out what strengths are there to animate its life for another year. The secret to its survival is found in how well it can draw from its roots.

For us as a school, that root is the charism of truth. It is strong and it is healthy and it is deep, but it is up to each of us to decide whether we will draw upon that founding charism and its practices or not.

Each of us here today is called to pursue truth with their whole heart, mind, and being, and to love it more than anything else. To search near and far, to take long journeys if necessary, in order to come face to face with it. Even when truth is unpleasant, we must not hide from it, but still desire to meet it and listen to what it has to say.

Even more challenging, each of us is called to say what we see as truthfully as we possibly can to the people who most need to know. Several years ago, Mike Stancil said to me, "Ann, you want your anger to be like a coursing stream, not a finely diffused mist." What he knew was that so often all of my frustration was dissipating in gossip and sarcasm with my friends rather than actually confronting the source. If we are to keep Veritas as our institutional motto, we owe it to each other to be honest with one another directly. To name the feelings. To share the impact. To ask the intent. To discover the assumptions. To find out there are pieces of the story we didn't know about. To offer the parts of the story the other didn't know.

And lastly, each of us is called to be true. To remain in relationship even when we might prefer wish not to be. To remain charitable and kind. Willing to assume the best motive in the other. Willing to initiate conversation again and again and again in loyalty to the person and the institution.

     Pursue truth
     Speak truthfully
     Be true.

It has been only gift for me to work side by side with Celeste these past six years. Everything that I have said today, I learned from the Gospel, but I experienced with her. And even though she leaves full-time service on our faculty, she does not leave the far-reaching community that is Aquinas Institute, and indeed she remains rooted in the charism of truth. Indeed she models what it means to draw from the roots better than anyone I know.

God speed, Celeste, to continue to
> Pursue truth
> Speak truthfully
> Be true.

33. Aquinas Midday Prayer
March 30, 2011
Deuteronomy 4: 1, 5-9

As many of you know, I like to spend Sunday mornings at College Church in the atrium for 9-12 year old children. Since returning from Christmas break, we've been reading together the book of Exodus, a little bit each week. It is such an amazing story. Foundational in so many ways to the entire Judeo-Christian tradition.

We've read about the oppression of the Israelites in Egypt and Moses' call to be the one to set them free. The children love the part about the plagues and the special Passover meal. We've looked at the map to find the Red Sea and pondered where they may have crossed it, and tried to trace their journey through the desert where they had to rely on God to meet even their most basic needs for food and for water. And, finally, we've read about how they arrive at Mt. Sinai for a dramatic meeting with God in which a once-in-human-history kind of covenant is made, knotted together with the gift of a law that will distinguish Israel from all other nations. After so many weeks, I am fairly familiar with the book of Exodus.

In preparation for preaching today, however, I found myself reading pretty large sections of the book of Deuteronomy, a book with which I am not terribly familiar. In reading, of course, I was immediately struck by how much Exodus and Deuteronomy have in common. They are both essentially about the same great event–the making of a mountaintop covenant between God and Israel, bound by the law. Indeed, the Hebrew title of "Deuteronomy"–"Mishnah Torah"–means "second account of the law" or "repeated law."

And yet, there are some very interesting differences.

In Exodus, when Moses ascends Mt. Sinai to receive God's commandments, he stays for forty days, and then returns down the mountain to share these commands with the people.

Deuteronomy seems to imply that when he came down from the mountain, he did not tell them what he had learned. Why is not clear. Perhaps like Mary, he took these things and pondered them in his heart.

Moses doesn't share the law he'd received until almost forty *years* later, when at the end of all their wandering, the Israelites have arrived at the edge of the Promised Land and Moses is on death's door.

Deuteronomy is written as Moses' great farewell speech, a sort of last will and testament in which he reflects on his time as their leader and what he wants them to remember. It is the same covenant he announces, a law grounded in the same ten central commandments. But there is a "distance" to it. Unlike Exodus, where God speaks in the present tense, in Deuteronomy, Moses relates what God said to him in the past, and there are some new ordinances and statutes that have been included – commandments that indicate this covenant has actually been pondered for far more than 40 years. Very practical, detailed commandments that indicate the people have some practice in trying to delineate what the law looks like in daily life for quite a while.

Most scholars think Deuteronomy was composed somewhere in the 7th century B.C., a couple hundred years after Exodus' version of the law was compiled, which was a couple hundred years after the original events that birthed the Exodus narrative took place.

By the time Deuteronomy was written down, the Israelite people had been trying to live covenant with God for centuries and had frequently failed miserably at it. They had insisted on having kings like other nations, kings who had been corrupt and abused the poor. They had been enchanted by other gods, influenced by neighboring cultures. In their jealousy and ill-will, they had split into two kingdoms, the northern one of which had recently been wiped out by the Assyrians, the southern one of which was suffering a massive wave of immigrants from the north. They had forgotten the once-in-human-history kind of relationship that they had forged with God, and it had not served them well.

And so one little scribe in Jerusalem, with perhaps a few companions, decided they need to tell the story again. They needed to help the people remember the covenant, remember their great falling in love with God on the mountaintop so long ago. They needed to tell the story of how it all began. They stitched together their memories and hid them in the temple where *someday, someone* could find them and re-kindle the flame... by *remembering.*

In the mouth of their most revered prophet of old, they placed these words of warning, words of pleading:

> "Take care and be earnestly on your guard
> not to forget the things which your own eyes have seen,
> nor let them slip from your memory as long as you live,
> but teach them to your children and to your children's children."

Don't forget. Remember.

In this third week of Lent, the daily lectionary readings call us repeatedly to remember the covenant, to return to the fundamental commitments of our life, to rekindle the love. Tomorrow, we'll hear Jeremiah talking about it ("Listen to my voice. Then I will be your God and you will be my people.") Friday and Saturday, we'll listen to the words of Hosea ("Return, O Israel")

Perhaps, the distinctive element that today's reading contributes to the week's theme is the important role that "telling the founding story" plays in rekindling that flame.

I remember a couple of years ago at a marriage workshop with Bridget Brennan, she asked each of the couples present to break away to a separate table and to remind each other of the story of how they met. Afterwards she said she can generally tell whether a couples' marriage will survive based on how animated and joyful they were when they remembered their founding story. She doesn't even need to be close enough to hear the story itself. Just from the front of the room, watching couples, she can tell. Telling the story rekindles the flame.

All of us here in the chapel today participate in covenant relationship. Through our baptism, we believe we have been grafted into a covenant relationship with God extended to us through Jesus Christ. Many of us probably don't quite remember the story of *that* day, but each of us in this chapel probably can recall the moment in which we truly became aware of what it meant to live out that covenant in a form of radical discipleship. We remember the moment we vowed our lives to a religious community. Or the moment we bound ourselves to Christian marriage. Or the time we turned our lives over to God saying "yes" in quite a decisive way to the vocation of ministry.

Remember for a moment that "yes."

Does it make you smile to think about it?

And when we grow weary and suffer defeats, when the vigor and zeal of our commitment has waned, and we've stumbled and fallen and forgotten…. perhaps it is time to write down again the story. To tell and share the story of how we first fell in love in quite an irreparable way.

The way we tell our covenant stories will change over time. Every time we tell it, we tell it in light of what we have learned since we made our promises. Highlighting different elements of the story that now stand out as keys for interpreting /foreshadowing the years that follow. That doesn't make it untrue. It makes it more true. It is part of the process—keeping the story alive for each new age, sparking a smile, igniting the love again.

This is what the "Anonymous Deuteronomists" did way back in the 7th century B.C. Their hidden text was found a century later in the temple under the reign of King Josiah and reignited a passion for the covenant among the Israelite people, resulting in a major reform and renewed energy to live the law again in a more vigorous way.

May our own remembering of our covenant stories this Lent do the same for us—rekindling the fire of love in us, returning us to the source of our life.

34. *Aquinas Midday Prayer*
September 7, 2011
Colossians 3:1-11

In my preparation for today, I want you to know that I went to the library and read *Sacra Pagina*, as all dutiful preachers should, but feeling a tad under-inspired, I also engaged in the dangerous activity of web surfing, googling "Colossians 3." The first entry that popped up read: *"The best Christians are dead Christians."*

Of course, I was shocked. Had my Google search accidentally steered me to some kind of religious hate site? How had typing in "Colossians 3" taken me here? And then I thought about it for a minute and started to laugh. Ultimately the link took me to—as you might guess—a dead end, but not before I was able to figure out this was the ingenious sermon title of an unknown pastor in a tiny town I've never heard of: "The best Christians are dead Christians."

The heart of Colossians 3, of course, is the mystery of Baptism as a type of dying—one of Paul's favorite mysteries, and naturally a favorite of all those who wrote in his name.

In our cozy Sunday morning parish baptisms today, with young doting parents nuzzling sweet faced infants in lacy white dresses passed on from Great Aunt Minnie, the notion of Baptism as death seems a bit foreign. But for Paul it was not; indeed it was central.

Baptism was a participation in the Paschal Mystery. The experience of going into the water was like a drowning. It was a dying with Christ, so that you could come out on the other side with Christ, leaving your old self behind. Some of the earliest baptismal fonts ever discovered, like the one at Dura Europas, hint at this—fashioned in the shape of a sarcophagi. Perhaps most explicit are the fonts found in Ethiopia—great crosses carved into the ground for the desiring Christian to walk down into and then walk up the other side.

I've often thought how disturbed Paul might be by many of the contemporary funeral memorial cards which mark the person's date of birth and then the date of "birth into eternal life" nearly a century later. "No! No! No!" Paul would have shouted, pulling at the roots of his thinning hair, "Your birth into eternal life is the date of your Baptism, *your Baptism.*" And to each of us he would gesticulate: "You! You! You are in your eternal life, NOW! You have been living your eternal life since the day you came out of the font."

And, of course, this is why the Colossians would have driven him nuts also. Because they didn't seem to be taking their baptism seriously. Didn't seem to remember that they were already in their eternal life... or, at least it was hard to tell by their actions toward one another.

And, so they needed a letter reminding them: *"The best Christians are dead Christians."*

The best Christians are those who've gone down into that font like it was a drowning and let their old habits die.
They've died to lying, died to anger, malice, and fury.
They've died to slander and gossip and saying nasty things about one another.

The best Christians are those who've died to their idols and immorality and impurity.

"The best Christians are dead Christians."

In the last verses from this passage, the Pauline author includes a few lines that sound very familiar:

> "Here there is not Greek and Jew,
> circumcision and uncircumcision,
> barbarian, Scythian, slave, free;
> but Christ is all, and in all"

These closing verses are almost identical to verses quoted elsewhere in the Pauline letters in Galatians and Corinthians. Scholars think that these verses may have been part of the Church's earliest Rite of Baptism—letting neophytes know that the Baptism they embrace will reshape their world, erasing all the strata of distinctions and hierarchies that mark every civilization. Again, Baptism mandates death to the status quo—not just at a personal level, but even at a societal one.

The pairings chosen in this particular version hint that some of the greatest struggles that the early Christian community at Colossae faced were ethnic in origin. They were having a hard time letting go of their own racial identities and not claiming privilege because of them; having a hard time treating newcomers as truly equal members of the Christian community. They were having a hard time letting old ways of looking at the world, inbred since birth, die so as to really see Christ in one another.

The best Christians, though, *are dead Christians*–they don't let such biases get in their way.

In many ways, today's poetic passage from Colossians can seem quite distant from us–reminiscent of another age, when Jews and Greeks really lived next door to each other, rather than only in lyrical verse. A time when Scythians actually existed and felt like a legitimate threat. A time when Baptism genuinely put one's life and livelihood at risk.

The danger, then, is that the passage might only emit a faint generic glow on the horizon of this new school year and never get very specific in our own lives.

So, let's go for shock value, like the unknown pastor from Anytown, and try on this phrase for size:
> "The best Aquinas Institute student is a dead Aquinas Institute student.
> The best A. I. faculty is a dead A.I. faculty,
> best A.I. president is a dead A.I. president."

Sounds positively dreadful, doesn't it? And, of course, I would like to make many caveats, but it does make us sit up straight in our chairs, doesn't it?

Each one of us here has been baptized and are here in this building out of response to that baptismal call. So, we can expect that here in this building we will be given many opportunities in this coming year to enter ever more fully into that baptism–dying to self, dying to what we thought would be, dying to how we thought the world was supposed to work.

I have no idea what that will look like for you or me this upcoming year:

Will it be learning to listen, really listen to someone from a group that I've grown up distaining, believing beneath my intellect?

Will it be overcoming a bias toward an author that you've dismissed in the past and argued against reading?

Will I find my anger surfacing again, just when I thought it had been put to sleep at last?

Will you come face-to-face with an idol you thought you had slain but you find out is still dictating your life?

I don't know what my baptism will ask me to die to this year, or what yours will ask of you... I only know that *it will ask*. And I pray that when it does ask, we will both have the sense to recognize: God wants to do something wonderful here, moving us through this death so that we can enjoy ever more fully the eternal life that is already ours, already in our grasp! If only we could let go of the old one.

35. *Aquinas Midday Prayer*
October 5, 2011
Jonah 4:1-11

The city of Mosul, Iraq lies quiet this morning–Inshallah.

It hasn't always been so, as you know. In the past decade we've woken up on any number of mornings to hear that another car bomb had been set off, more police recruits were dead, the U.S. was launching another offensive.

One particularly frightening morning five years ago, we woke up to hear that a bomb had detonated in front of the Dominican "Clock" church–a central Christian presence in Mosul since 1872. The Dominicans, of course, have been there even longer. They went at the request of Pope Benedict – Pope Benedict the *Fourteenth*, that is, in the year 1750.

They were sent to serve the Christian community of the region, which then, as now, is primarily Assyrian in heritage, intermingled among the Muslim Kurds and Arabs and Turkomen.

If we were with our Dominican brothers and sisters this fine morning, they might take us to a large hill in the city, across the Tigris River from the heart of the modern-day Mosul.

It is a hill they call Nebi Yūnus, located amidst the archeological ruins of an ancient city once known as the capital of a vast Assyrian empire– the city Nineveh.

There are two hills on this side of the river, actually. The other Kuyunjik–or Shepherd's Hills–has benefited from tremendous archeological exploration over the past couple decades. Remnants of a palace have been found there, once inhabited by King Sennacherib. Amazing relief sculptures were discovered as part of the dig, though many of these were destroyed in the fighting of 2003.

Nebi Yūnus, in contrast, has remained largely untouched by the archeologists. It is considered a sacred site, with memories considered more precious, and hence, more untouchable than those of palaces. Here there is a large mosque, built atop an old Nestorian Christian church, built atop the rumored tomb of Nebi Yūnus—the prophet Jonah—though no one has ever dug down deep enough to see if there are bones there.

Legend has it that this is the hill east of the old city walls that Jonah climbed on that quiet morning we find in today's reading.

The quiet morning after the noisy afternoon when he had walked through the boulevards of this most powerful city and told the people they were damned to extinction if they did not change their ways.

The quiet morning after a night of wailing and gnashing of teeth in which the Assyrian king pleaded on the peoples' behalf and promised repentance.

The quiet morning after God changed God's mind, and Jonah felt hung out to dry.

Legend has it that this is the hill where Jonah and God had the kind of talk that only Jewish prophets are allowed to get away with.

Abraham Heschel, in his work on the prophets, noted that the prophets are friends of the Lord. They are so intimate with God that they feel what God feels, speak what God speaks, concern themselves with what God concerns Godself.

So close are they to God that sometimes God seeks *their* counsel.
So close are they that their conversations can occasionally resemble lovers' spats: "You duped me!" shouts Jeremiah. "You've stuck me in the desert with a bunch of crazy stubborn people!" complains Moses.

But never did God have so feisty a friend as in the prophet Yūnus.

"I *knew* it!" he cries. "I *knew* it! I tried to flee from you and sail to Tarshish because I knew you were a softy. Look, when I tried to run away, you saved *me*. And now, when these Assyrians promise to change their ways, you decide to save *them*."

As Jack Sasson, the author of the *Anchor Bible Commentary* on Jonah "ventriloquizes,"

"Even as the seas were raging, even as I was falling into the gaping mouth of a fish, I knew you to be full of bluster; when eyeball to eyeball, as usual you blinked first...

"[And] God, now that you know how I really feel about this whole experience, you can go ahead and kill me; erase, if you dare, that miracle you performed in the sea for me."

But God doesn't smite him.

Indeed God seems to have a special soft spot for #4's on the Enneagram, every last one of them.

And God goes very gentle with Jonah.

Like a guy who brings home flowers to his aggrieved spouse, God brings Jonah a *qiqayon*–often translated, a gourd plant, though gourd plants don't actually do the kinds of things this plant can do – grow at the speed of lightening, produce shade in a day's time. This plant is another miracle, but more than that, it is also a parable. God wants to use it to gently teach Jonah about how much each and every life means to Him. If Jonah can fall in love with a big gourd plant and be so distressed over its decay, isn't God allowed to get attached to the 120,000 Assyrians of Nineveh.... *Not to mention their cows?*

And, on that rather humorous line, the book of Jonah ends. Not just the chapter, the whole book.

The reader wants to say, "What?! You've got to be kidding me. Cows? What's that about? What happens next?

Does Jonah get over being made a fool of–having to prophesy something that doesn't actually come true (the very worst thing that can happen to a prophet really)?

Does God coax him down off that hilltop?

Or does he break off the friendship, convinced that God just used him as a pawn and really cares about the Assyrians more than him?

In despair, does he simply die there on that hill?

Well, what do you think? It strikes me that whenever texts end this way, it is not because the author has just run out of ink. No, the author wants to get us talking, wants us to continue the story, wants us to form an opinion about how things end.

So, I invite you to consider for a moment about what you think happened next between God and Jonah. What is your intuition?

Does God blink again or call down a bolt of lightning?
Does Jonah cultivate the grudge or move on?
Does Jonah live or does he die right here?
Are there bones under where we are standing on this hill in Mosul or not?
What does your experience of friendship and fighting with God tell you about these things?

Jews and Muslims, of course, have their suspicions, arising out of their experiences of friendship with God. One medieval midrash claims that, "At that very moment, Jonah fell flat on his face saying, 'Direct your world according to the attribute of mercy, as is written, 'Mercy and forgiveness belong to the Lord our God." Another has him meeting the prophet Elijah while staying with his mother, the widow of Zarephath. When Jonah died, God raised him again from the dead through Elijah, for he wanted to show him that "it is not possible to run away from God."

Alongside these stories, it seems important to note that there is *another* mosque in Hallul, about 2 miles from Hebron in the West Bank that also purports to be the tomb of Jonah, as well as a Jewish site near Sarepta in Lebanon. Jonah's ongoing relationship with God is clearly an open-ended question in these traditions as well.

I have my own suspicions, of course.

I suspect God told Jonah that he'd not been a pawn for the salvation of the Assyrians at all. Rather, perhaps the Assyrians had been the pawn for the salvation of Jonah, facilitating a conversion Jonah needed to have—so that Jonah could see with his very own eyes that people really *can* change, that repentance *is* possible, and that God *is* mercy.

I lean in this direction because this is how God has frequently worked with me. Sent me somewhere thinking I had something important to teach, while slowly making me realize I had something to learn.

As to where he is buried, I have no idea, but I like to think it might be this hill in Mosul. Not because I want Jonah to have died there in despair on that day, but because it is lovely to think of Jonah continuing to live among the Assyrians—a new friendship emerging out of the realization that each of them had found their salvation in their encounter with the other.

I like to think Jonah settled among them, and those cows that God loved so much, and discovered for himself that God's love was big enough to embrace them all, without anyone feeling shortchanged.

I like to think that friendship between the jilted children of God could happen again here.

I like to think that this Nebi Yūnus could be a meeting ground.

I like to think that Mosul will be quiet for many years to come—inshallah.

The entire book of Jonah is only 689 words.

I like to think that word we shall write in slot 690 is shalom, salem, peace.

36. *Aquinas Midday Prayer*
September 5, 2012
Luke 4: 38-44

My 11-year-old nephew Max has been having nightmares about the Parousia.

So reports my sister (Max's mom) who called me a few weeks ago to report this.... And to wonder what the &$! I've been telling him in atrium this past year. (It might help to know that I've been Max's Sunday catechist for the past several years.)

"Really? He's scared of the Parousia?" I asked her. "How would he have gotten afraid of the Parousia?"

"Ann, I don't even what the Parousia *is*," she said, "so it didn't happen in my house."

I explained to her that the Parousia *is* something we talk about a lot in the atrium. It is the final moment in the history of the Kingdom of God
.... Another way of talking about where time is headed,
... What earth will look like when all God's dreams for our planet are realized.
... In Corinthians, St. Paul says it'll be the day when "God will be all in all."

Every time we talk about it in the atrium, the children get very excited about it. You see, every child seems to have planted within them the seed of the Kingdom of God–a strong belief that the world is supposed to be better than it is, and that their generation is going to make it so. This seed seems to flower in a particular way in the pre-adolescent. Often when we pray together, someone in Max's group will pray, "God, make the Parousia come fast." They want it that much.

But it is also true that sometimes kids hear other things about "The End of Time" on the playground, in the movies. The Mayan Calendar has certainly popped up in their conversation in the last couple months. The exploding sun is a perennial topic.

"Let me talk to him," I said. "Let him come with me to clean up the atrium for the coming year."

And so this past Sunday, Max and I got together with some rags and Windex up in our sacred space at College Church. And while we were dusting, I said to him, "Max, here is a work I don't think you've seen before. It has some of the clues the prophets gave us when they were trying to describe what the Parousia will look like. I need you to help me check it and make sure all the pieces are still here."

Inside the box is a set of 12 scripture cards (mostly from the book of Isaiah) that match up with different themes related to the Parousia. Slowly Max read them and placed them.

"Then will the eyes of the blind be opened and the ears of the deaf unstopped. The lame will leap like a deer and the tongue of the mute shout for joy."

"They will beat their swords into plowshares, and their spears into pruning hooks."

"The wolf will live with the lamb, the leopard will lie down with the goat."

"Your sons and daughters will prophesy, your old men will dream dreams, your young men will see visions."

The readings went on. When he finished, we sat and talked for a while about his favorites, which ones he might like to draw a picture of... about how the Parousia was something we look forward to; nothing to fear. He especially likes the idea of all of the animals being in harmony with each other and there not being allergies to any of them anymore.

As we were putting the cards away, he said, "You know this has happened before."

"When?" I asked.

"Jesus," he said.

Today's Gospel from Luke constitutes, in the words of one scripture scholar, "A Typical Day in the Life of Jesus." He prays, he preaches, he heals, he eats, he heals some more, he exorcises demons, and he moves on. Wherever he goes, he talks about this mystery of the Kingdom of God, of what God dreams for planet Earth. But more than that, wherever he goes, the Kingdom of God starts breaking out. Little snapshots of the Parousia flashing in history.

- people who were enemies conversing and eating with one another
- people who were blind now able to see
- the deaf able to hear
- those who couldn't walk now able to pick up their mats and go home
- strange spirits moving through the land prophesying

Wherever Jesus goes, he doesn't just talk to people about the Kingdom, they get to experience it. Jesus is the one in whom God *is* "all in all"– and so where he is, the Parousia is.

Sometimes in a modern culture we have a hard time "getting" the miracle stories in scripture. We get wrapped up in questions of science– what really happened? Was it natural or supernatural? Why doesn't it happen today? Or we get wrapped up in questions of theodicy–why this person and not that person? What role does faith have to play in who gets healed or not? If I prayed more, believed more, would I get a miracle? Or we focus on the disability–what is wrong with being deaf? Maybe is that not a gift rather than a curse?

These are all fair questions, but I wonder if they aren't slightly off target. Maybe what the Gospel writer most wants us to know is that the Kingdom of God is real. God does have a plan for us. And in those places / those persons saturated with God – where God is "all in all"– sometimes the Parousia busts through. Just starts to happen.

Max and I began to wonder whether there weren't other people who seemed to have a Parousia bubble around them wherever they go. He pulled out the saint book we have on the shelf with St. Francis on the cover–a wolf at his side and birds on his shoulders all living in harmony. And the picture of St. Martin de Porres and his mice. St. Elizabeth with her aprons of multiplying bread. Sts. Peter and John with the man begging at the temple gate.

"Have you actually seen any Parousia people?" I asked Max.

"No," he said. But then talked about a teacher he really liked, in whose class everyone gets along—even those kids who don't like each other.

And I thought about people I know who have "wiped away every tear" from my eyes, people who've taught me how to live in peace rather than wage my own little wars, people who've healed just by their presence.

"I think I'd like to be one of those people," I said, "Someone who is so filled with God that the Parousia just starts happening."

"One time a butterfly came and just sat on my shoulder," he said.

"Sound like maybe you've already experienced a little hint of Parousia then, haven't you?"

"Mmmhmm"

"Imagine how amazing—when everything and everyone is filled to the brim with God."

"Mmmhmm"

"I wonder if it is going to break out somewhere this week."

"Maybe"

Go to all the other towns and proclaim the good news of the Kingdom of God.

37. *Aquinas Midday Prayer*
September 26, 2012
Proverbs 30:5-9

For as long as I can remember, I've been familiar with what might be called "the three wishes joke." I'm sure you are, too. That joke with infinite variations in which a person (or persons) is granted three wishes for anything they want, often by a genie that has been released from a lantern. The first two wishes are usually brilliant and then are somehow undone by the third one.

Like the three men on a deserted island who are granted such an opportunity. The first wished to go to Paris and "poof" he is standing in front of the Eifel Tower. The second wished to go Hawaii and "poof" he is dancing hula in Waikiki. The third man sighs, "I'm lonely…I wish my friends were back."

Of course, sometimes the first two wishes are not so brilliant either. We could recount the Irish version of the poor couple. The wife was so surprised at the genie's invitation she said the first thing that came to mind: "I want a sausage." The husband, in anger that his wife hadn't asked for a fortune or a bigger farm, wished that the sausage get stuck up her nose. They had to use up the third wish to get it out.

In every version, the person ends up exactly where they began, no better… and sometimes for the worse.

Perhaps this is why—in our passage from Proverbs – the protagonist (a man that scripture names as Agur, but about whom it says no more) only asks two wishes. Two things that he wants more than anything else before he dies. And, as we might suspect from a section of the Bible called "wisdom literature," the two choices are neither foolish nor wasted, but really worthy ones:

First, he wants the truth… "Put falsehood and lying far from me."

And, second, he wants to be in the middle class. I realize it sounds a little odd when put that way. He says it a bit more elegantly: "Give me neither poverty nor riches; provide me only with the food I need; lest being full, I deny you, saying, 'Who is the LORD?' Or, being in want, I steal, and profane the name of my God."

I know as a community we have thought about Truth before. Indeed, I think it may have come up in my own conversations here at Aquinas once or twice.

So I was intrigued when reflecting on this passage to spend some time with the second of the wishes—especially because it is linked to themes that have so dominated the news in recent months with the Recession and Occupy Wall Street and the 1% and now the 47%.

The Christian tradition gives us a lot of mixed messages about right relationship with wealth. We definitely have a Gospel record that lifts up freely-chosen poverty as virtuous, even essential for true discipleship, and names the poor as dearest to God's heart. Think of the camel trying to get through the needle's eye or Lazarus begging at the gate. Wealth is considered dangerous, even damning. Jesus commands the rich young man to sell all he has and follow. The fox and lair have their nests, but the Son of Man has no place to lay his head.

At the same time, we have a two thousand year old lived experience that includes magnificent palaces and art collections, endowed institutions... and weekly bingo gatherings. Some of which have admittedly not been good for the Church, but a lot of which probably have.

Even those of us who take vows of poverty, generally aren't really poor—in the sense of having no security, no resources, no idea of where to get a next meal. It might be better to say that we have committed to living simply, because real poverty, as we've seen highlighted in study after study – is a morally hazardous place to be –decreasing human dignity, increasing violence, decreasing life expectancy, increasing abortion. Just this past week, I was listening to a story on NPR about the effects of poverty on children's brain development—how they can directly correlate increase of adrenalin due to constant stress to decreased capacity to learn and retain information in school.

Which brings us back to the insights of Agur that pre-date even our own Christian tradition: the recognition that both "too much" and "too little" are dangerous to human flourishing. We definitely could identify truly poor persons who have become great saints and rich men who have walked through the eye of the needle. But most of us find the healthiest place to be spiritually as well as physically is somewhere in between. A place where we can grow neither too arrogant nor too desperate.

Of course one of the more pressing issues of our age, as any age, is to figure out what that "right amount" looks like. We might all agree that we want to live "in moderation" but when the conversation moves to trying to pin numbers to Agur's wish, one can quickly end up with a sausage up the snozzle as we've seen in so many political debates of late. What kind of income does a family of four need each year? $20,000; $40,000; $60,000; $80,000? Should we budget in the costs of Catholic education? Of college? Location? How about a single person? How about a non-profit institution?

It gets really complicated really fast. Kudos go to ethicists like Julie Rubio over at SLU who have given this question real and sustained thought–not just platitudes like "live simply, share one's resources." One of the more interesting statistics I read in her most recent book is that U.S. Christians (Protestant & Catholic combined) give an average of 3% of their income to charity–total. It would seem mysteriously like none of us feels like our cup truly "overfloweth."

Agur's proverb seems so simple and straightforward, but it is not.

So here is a question for you today. Let's say that you believe today's scripture–that you agree with Agur that a life somewhere between "too much" and "too little" is to be aspired to. And then, let's pretend that when you go back to your office after lunch, a genie squiggles out of your incense burner (because that's about as close to magic lanterns as we get at Aquinas) and says to you, "Hey, that last wish you made was a little vague. How about I give you one more? A chance to clarify what it is that you really have in mind.

Tell me, what is the food *you* need?
How would you know if you had too much?
How would you know if you had too little?
And what would it look like if you had "just right"?
Would your life be any different than it is now?
Talk to me about how.

And remember, don't give an answer too fast. You don't want a sausage up your nose. You don't want to end up back where you began...

unless, of course, you decide that you do. Consider carefully what it would mean to live out Agur's last wish today.

38. *Aquinas Midday Prayer*
November 28, 2012
Luke 21:5-19

Given the season of the year we are in (with Christ the King having just passed us by and Advent right around the corner) my initial reading of today's Gospel from Luke led me to clump it with similar passages from Mark and Matthew about "The End Times" – what it will look like just before God wraps up history once and for all.

I learned something new, though, when reading the exegetical commentary on this text. Something that is, of course, obvious if one slows down to read carefully – which (I am embarrassed to admit) I hadn't done before. The "something" is that Luke's Jesus isn't talking here about the end of time at all, but the end of the Temple in Jerusalem. An event that had taken place in 70 A.D., about twenty years before Luke put pen to parchment.

Luke wants us to know that Jesus was a trustworthy prophet, much like Jeremiah was a trustworthy prophet when he stood in the midst of the Temple hundreds of years earlier and predicted that it would fall, just before it did... the first time. Jesus, like Jeremiah, doesn't tell people what they want to hear; he tells them the truth. And, the things Jesus said would happen *had* happened in the decades between Jesus' preaching and Luke's writing. There *had* been wars and earthquakes. Rome *had* devastated the city, despite all the false leaders that had tried to rouse the people to revolt against the empire and promised they could triumph.

More than that, in the years preceding the fall, Jesus' disciples themselves had been under attack. They'd been arrested and imprisoned. They'd been betrayed by their families and hauled before authorities with suspicion. How do we know? Because Luke also wrote the book of Acts. And all the things Jesus is saying here in chapter 21 run parallel to the adventures he records about the early Church in the season just before the Temple fell.

The point that seems important here is that Jesus isn't talking about what life will look like at the end of time, but in the Church's time…which sounds pretty dreadful, granted… but also is not "The End."

I remember many moons ago when I was taking Church History with Ginger Peters, and each era we studied seemed worse that the last. Ginger would say, "Well, this was a particularly dark and dangerous era for the Church." But she said it so often that one day in class we finally confronted her, "Ginger, you say that every week. *Every* century sounds like a dark and dangerous time in the life of the Church." And she laughed and admitted, "Well, now that you mention it!"

There are still earthquakes and wars, famines and persecutions. Families are still divided down the middle on politics and religion, and continue to betray their members in horrible ways on a regular basis. False prophets still abound, feeding on peoples' deepest longings and worst biases. Is our century any worse than the last twenty? Two semesters of Ginger's Church history would not lead me to think so. Is it any better? I doubt that, too.

So perhaps the existence of such events is not really Jesus' point here. Maybe the more important focus in the text is what comes next. After listing all these dreadful things, Jesus says something really intriguing:

"This will give you an opportunity to testify."

Here is where I found myself sitting for a while and wondering. In Luke's Gospel, it is almost as if all the crashing and burning sets the stage for the preacher to arrive and give a word. What word? Why only then?

And here I have to move from the big, global picture of massive natural disasters and ceaseless war… to down here, close in, micro-level. I don't even want to try here to justify the grandeur of evil on the large scale – suffering so vast it defies comprehension. I'll leave that to the systematicians.

My wonderings are more immediate, more personal. In what way have the cataclysmic events of our times, prepared *me* to *receive* testimony? In what way have the cataclysmic events of my life (small though they may be in the grand scheme of things) prepared *me* to *give* testimony? And what kind of testimony have they prepared me to give?

I know for myself, there is something about suffering that readies me to listen to another person's testimony. The fact that *I* have suffered makes me hungry–even desperate–for answers in a way that I wasn't before. The fact that *they* have suffered makes them more trustworthy, more credible a witness to me. Why do we sit at the feet of Desmond Tutu? Trip over ourselves to catch a glimpse of the Dalai Lama? Strain to hear the quiet voice of Immaculee Ilibagiza? Because they have witnessed earthquakes and famines, wars, and persecutions by their own people... and we believe they have something to say that they may not have otherwise. As Jesus says, these events have prepared us to listen and to talk in a new way.

But, about what? What is the testimony?

Here is where I think we must be most careful. For, Jesus seems to say that you can't prepare for all that life has to hand you; nor can you prepare in advance what you are going to say about it. There is no canned message here Jesus gives to his disciples. No talking points.

He only says: Don't prepare your defense in advance. Don't interpret things before they happen. Only God can give us the wisdom we'll need, and only at the moment in which we will need it. Words come like daily bread. We can't collect them for tomorrow, lest they become stale and rotten like stored manna. And, I'm guessing you've tasted stale words coming to you from the pulpit before. Words you suspect have not been lived, have not been tried, have not been tested. When what you are looking for is words that are true. Words that the preacher doesn't just "know" *about* (in the head) but "*knows*" (in the gut).

So experiment with me for one moment here, because–like Luke's community so long ago–I know every person here in this chapel is aware of the cataclysmic events going on in our world today, and– moreover–in his or her own personal life has suffered. I've heard your petitions week after week. You know what it is like to have loved and to have lost; to have your faith be a source of friction in your life. You know about family divisions and betrayal. You, too, have seen temples fall that you thought could never crumble. You may not live in The End of Time, but you do live in the Church's time.

And I wonder, "What is the testimony that you would offer today? What word do you want to give to a world that knows such grief?" It doesn't have to be something you'd say for forever. It doesn't have to apply everywhere and always or be the definitive, singular answer to the vast sufferings of our world. It might be a word just for today, the wisdom of God for this place at this time in our struggles, and that is okay.

But the world needs you to give it. Now is your opportunity. And so, what is the testimony you have to bear? And where could you share it today?

39. *Aquinas Midday Prayer*
February 27, 2013
Matthew 20:17-28

I came upon her the morning after along the riverbank, beating the last remnants of dirt and color out of a thin piece of cloth with a rock and then rinsing them down stream. I'd heard from Mark that her name was Salome but I did not dare address her by her first name. For, she was a very traditional woman wedded to Zebedee and the culture of her time, so she didn't really have a name and thought that *appropriate*.

When I spotted her, even from a distance, I recognized I'd seen her before... No, maybe she just looked like someone else I knew. Well, you know, come to think of it, she looked kind of like Mary of Nazareth. Maybe the old apocrypha really was true and they *were* sisters–which would make a little more sense as to why she'd been so brazen yesterday: Going up to Jesus like that and asking that *her* two sons–and hers only–be seated at Jesus' right and left hand in the Kingdom. If they were related, well–again, it would only be *appropriate*.

It wasn't that she didn't want to see changes. Oh no, she did. You could hear it in the cracking of one rock against another and the vigor with which she wrung excess water from the twisted garment. She despised the Romans like all of her neighbors. She despised the corruption in her own peoples' leaders–the extortion and wastefulness more befitting foreigners than those set apart to be a light to the nations. She was one who had waited in sincere hope for the coming of the Messiah who would set her people free while so many of the religious leaders in Jerusalem only gave the aspiration lip service.

And Jesus.... Jesus had that magnetic charisma, that born-leader quality that could make change happen. Hadn't she been one of the first to spot it? Hadn't she been one to encourage him to dream dreams since his childhood? When others had scoffed–"What good could come from Nazareth? Really, a carpenter's son?"–hadn't she defended him before the naysayers. Hadn't she encouraged her sons to go with him, even if it meant she and Zebedee were left alone for long periods of time in their old age. Was it really too much to ask that her Jimmy and her Johnny get key positions in his coming administration? Isn't it only *appropriate* that those roles should go to the people who've been with you from the very beginning?

But things had not gone the way she'd planned. No, not at all. She'd waited for what she thought was just the right moment to make the ask, but then, instead of a simple "yes," Jesus answered.... Well, he didn't answer *her*, that was for sure. It was like she wasn't even there and all hell broke loose. Her sons were shamed and Jesus' band of men all started arguing with one another. And she.... She slunk away without anyone noticing, and now even her sons weren't talking to her. "Woman," their eyes seemed to say, "What'd you go and do *that* for?"

After a while, she threw the garment into a bucket and sat back on her haunches, elbows resting on knees staring into the river. I was afraid she might turn around and see me, and if that happened I wouldn't be quite sure what to say, so I was considering slinking off myself when I noticed that Jesus was drawing near her and also squatting down along side her.

"Auntie," he said.

She rose to her full height of 5 ft. 2–and turned to look down on him, her eyes flashing with anger and hurt: "I don't understand you. We have been without any power over our lives for so long. You could change that. You could make things different for us if you were in charge."

"Auntie," he said again, "You want to work the system. I want to break the system. You want to keep the game and just change the players. I want to rewrite the rules of the game."

"Well, what is stopping you? I'm waiting. I've been waiting for a long time for the world to be different."

"Well, certainly the guys over there are not the quickest of learners, as I needed to explain to them again yesterday. But quite frankly, Auntie, one of the things that is also making it difficult is people like you," he said.

"Me!" she exclaimed with outrage. "Me! I am an old woman who has worked hard her whole life and have not a shekel to show for it. I am entirely dependent on my husband and two grown sons to take care of me, and those sons are currently unemployed, apparently with dim future prospects. How can *I* be the problem? I don't even own a name."

"My point precisely. The system is stacked against you, but it only works if you agree to keep it working."

"And *how*, pray tell, do *I* agree to keep it working?"

"By assenting to the fact that power is to be feared and that others call the shots. By agreeing that titles mean something and treating people differently when they have one. By consenting that your basic needs can only be provided by men. By assuming that when you are told something the only possible response is 'okay.' By sulking away and swallowing your anger rather than speaking it. By not asking questions when you see something you think is unfair. By not demanding that you have your own name....When you do these things – whether you mean to or not – you are keeping the system alive & well."

"But not to do so is very dangerous and I want to survive."

"Well, now we arrive at the truth. I, honestly, would rather die than do these things."

"Don't say it. Don't...."

Only at this point did he stand up. "Auntie, do not worry. I will show you how to do it right."

"So who really *is* going to sit on your right and your left?" she asked.

"You're asking the wrong question," he said.

"So you've made clear, but I'm just really curious."

"Some tiny Indian woman who hasn't been born yet and a crazy beggar dude from the mountains of Italy."

"Oh, okay," she said, looking confused. I wondered if she would stay with him now that her hopes had been dashed, her game board ripped in two. I wondered if maybe she might just leave James and John to their own fate and retire to the comfort of Zebedee's protection for her remaining days.   But as Jesus walked away, something of a smile crossed her face, even as a tear rolled down from the corner of her eye.

And then I knew where I'd seen her before. At the tomb, on the third day. She was one of those Easter morning women with courage strong enough to go out in the deep darkness before dawn armed only with spices,... strong enough to confront soldiers and rocks three times her size.

40. *Aquinas Midday Prayer*
May 1, 2013
John 15: 1-8

(This was my last time to preside at midday prayer before departing from the regular Aquinas faculty.)

This past Saturday, we buried my Uncle Mike–who I know that many of you have heard me pray for week after week this semester. Even though he was married to my aunt for almost forty years and I was in their wedding as flower girl at the tender age of five, I wouldn't say I knew him particularly well. But what I do know is the way my aunt and my cousins hung with him even as he diminished before our eyes, first losing the right side of his jaw and then part of his lung, his hair, his eyebrows, his strength, his vigor, his vitality, and finally, his hope for any sort of recovery.

When there was really nothing more that could be done, it frustrated some of us–can't we bring more food, more prayers, more fuzzy blankets? No, the freezer, linen closet, and even spiritual bouquet were stocked.

When I brought his daughter from the airport last week, she walked into the bedroom and said, "Is there anything you need, Dad?" and he simply pointed to the space next to him in the bed. She lay down at his side and put her head on his shoulder. "Closer," he said. She scootched more. "Closer," he said again. "I can't," she stated, "or I'd be right on top of you and I don't want to hurt you." "I'd be okay with that," he said as a tear rolled down his cheek. And a tear rolled down hers.

I've thought about this moment a lot in the past week. In the end, we don't want blankets and food, or even–dare I say–prayers. What we want is those we love close to us. So close that they become one with us. We can't get them close enough. The deepest human desire is not for stuff, even the basic stuff we need to stay alive and comfortable. Truly, the deepest human desire is for communion. To love and to be loved; to dwell in love.

Is it really any surprise that Jesus would express this desire himself on the night before he died? There were no more trips to the temple to take. No more fishing expeditions on the Sea of Galilee to be had. No more "calling" and "following" and "inviting 'Come!" His last request / his deepest desire was that we simply remain with Him, in Him.

It seems like such a simple thing–just remain…. Really? That's all you want me to do–just be with you? Rest with you? Rest in you? Not serve you? Not make great sacrifices for you? Not move mountains for you? Really, just "remain" in you?

Simple indeed… That is until you try it. At which point we discover that "remaining" is among the most difficult activities that one can ever undertake. Sometimes it can be an immensely pleasurable activity, just to be in the presence of someone you love and spend time with them. But it also requires the capacity to still be there, even when you are bored of looking into their eyes and bored of hearing them tell the same story for the umpteenth time and would rather be watching TV or attacking your massive to-do list.

And sometimes it requires staying in the same room when you are so angry with them you could spit. It means continuing to talk and to share your feelings even when they are ugly and tangled and it'd be easier to create a wall of silence twelve feet thick.

And sometimes–as I saw last week–remaining means you will see people you love in tremendous pain and that is *such* an uncomfortable place to be…. Or it means *being seen* in all one's weakness and vulnerability and need, which for some of us is probably the hardest of all.

We often talk as if "going" requires the greatest strength. We admire those who run marathons and travel to faraway, exotic places– sacrificing life and limb to conquer the frontiers of human capacity. But, truthfully, the greater strength is not in going; it is in remaining.

And unless we nurture the capacity for remaining in ourselves, we will never taste the communion that every fiber of our being longs for. We will conquer the highest mountains and the greatest distances but we will still be hungry. Because at the very core of our beings, communion is what we were created for. In short, we will never bear fruit.

We might do incredible activities. We might be outrageously busy. But–in the words of the great Dominican Dalmazio Mongillo–these good works will be like ornaments hung on a Christmas tree, rather than fruit blossoming on a vine.

Now you might wonder what business I have preaching on the virtues of remaining when I myself am in the process of packing up and moving from St. Louis. Yes, that irony has not gone unnoticed by me. But, the remaining that Jesus talks about I think has little to do with space. It has to do with fidelity to relationships despite distances, expanses of time, even the boundaries of death. One of the most beautiful doctrines in all Catholic teaching is that of the communion of saints which says that all of us who have the sap of the Spirit running through our veins are forever linked whether we live here or there, now or then, living or dead.

This past Sunday when I was meditating on this parable with the children in the atrium, one of the things they emphasized about vines is that, unlike trees, they are not space bound. The nature of a vine is to spread. And in their artwork of the true vine, they often draw the vine circling the whole earth.

A few years ago, a Mexican catechist of the Good Shepherd named Maria Christlieb (who had spent much time meditating on these verses with children) died of cancer, and these words were found written by her hand next to her bed when she died. I want to close with them because they have repeatedly come to mind as I consider the invitation to "remain" in my own life right now. Perhaps they will speak to you, too. She wrote:

> "It is not a question now of saying 'yes' or 'no'; it is enough to say I will remain. How one remains is not important; it is enough to say I will remain... The Vinedresser called me at the first hour; the Vine is the history: He, making it; I, remaining in Him. After all the crises that I have lived, God has always had a surprise prepared for me. Today I say that I will remain with the hope of the surprise he has for me. It just means continuing to work with God in another way in history and remaining."

Amen, Maria. Amen.

The Author

Ann Garrido is associate professor of homiletics at Aquinas Institute of Theology in St. Louis, MO where she served as a regular faculty member and program administrator from 2000–2013. She preached regularly at the school. *Preaching to the Choir* includes forty selections of Garrido's preaching, providing a window into the way the Word of God intersects with very particular events in the community's history and the author's own life.

She now continues teaching with the institute from a distance while also working as a consultant in the areas of conflict mediation, administration, and leadership development. She is the author of three other books: *Mustard Seed Preaching* (LTP, 2004); *A Concise Guide to Supervising a Ministry Student* (Ave Maria, 2008); and *Redeeming Administration* (Ave Marian, 2013), as well as numerous journal and magazine articles.

28826599R00094

Made in the USA
Charleston, SC
23 April 2014